Making Books

That Fly, Fold, Wrap, Hide, Pop Up, Twist & Turn

Books for Kids to Make

Making Books

That Fly, Fold, Wrap, Hide, Pop Up, Twist & Turn

Gwen Diehn

LARK CRAFTS
Asheville

Editor: Deborah Morgenthal
Art Director and Production: Kathleen J. Holmes
Production assistance: Bobby Gold
Illustrations: Gwen Diehn
Photography: Evan Bracken

An Imprint of Sterling Publishing
387 Park Avenue South
New York, NY 10016

If you have questions or comments about
this book, please visit: larkcrafts.com

The Library of Congress has cataloged the hardcover edition as follows:

Diehn, Gwen, 1943-
    Making books that fly, fold, wrap, hide, pop up, twist, & turn :
book for kids to make / Gwen Diehn.
    Includes index.
    ISBN 1-57990-023-2
    1. Toy and movable books—Design—Juvenile literature.
  [1. Handicraft.   2. Toy and movable books—Design.]   I. Title.
  Z1033.T68D54   1998
  736'.98—dc21   97-41037

10 9 8 7 6

Published by Lark Crafts
An Imprint of Sterling Publishing Co., Inc.
387 Park Avenue South, New York, NY 10016

First Paperback Edition 2006
© 1998, Gwen Diehn

Distributed in Canada by Sterling Publishing,
c/o Canadian Manda Group, 165 Dufferin Street
Toronto, Ontario, Canada M6K 3H6

Distributed in the United Kingdom by GMC Distribution Services,
Castle Place, 166 High Street, Lewes, East Sussex, England BN7 1XU

Distributed in Australia by Capricorn Link (Australia) Pty Ltd.,
P.O. Box 704, Windsor, NSW 2756 Australia

Manufactured in China

ISBN 13: 978-1-57990-023-6 (hardcover) 978-1-57990-326-8 (paperback)

For information about custom editions, special sales, and premium and
corporate purchases, please contact Sterling Special Sales Department
at 800-805-5489 or specialsales@sterlingpub.com.

Requests for information about desk and examination copies
available to college and university professors must be submitted
to academic@larkbooks.com. Our complete policy can be found
at www.larkcrafts.com.

Contents

INTRODUCTION

This is a book about making books. Many of you have already made books for stories that you have written or to use as journals or notebooks. This book will help you take the making of books a step further. Most people think of a book as something that holds or contains whatever is written or drawn in it, and many books are just that. But the books that this book will help you make are more than that—they will actually be a part of the message they contain, and their very design will make the message better, clearer, stronger.

Books as containers, books as messages—what would you say a book is anyway? We all know the simple answer: a book is a bunch of written on or printed on pieces of paper glued or stitched together in such a way that the pages turn, and one or two pages at a time can be seen and read.

But wait—what about Japanese accordion-folded books? Are these books, even though the pages are glued together into one very long page, which is then folded? What about books that have no writing or printing but are full of pictures? Can you call that a book? Can you call something a book if it unfolds like a map and its pages are individual cards that can be slipped into little pockets in one order or another, depending on how you want the story to turn out?

Can you call it a book if it's big enough to walk through? How about a book that is small enough to be carried in a little pouch that hangs from your belt? Have you ever seen a book made up of five kites, each with part of a poem written on it? Or a book that looks like a window shade, with each page working like one of the slats? The people of Indonesia had books like that a long time ago, and they called them *palm leaf* books.

Can a book be one long piece of paper rolled into a scroll? The early Egyptians and certain Native Americans thought so. Does a book even have to be made out of paper? Many early scroll books were made out of animal skins or tree bark. How about a book in which each page is a thin piece of ivory? The ancient Chinese made some books like this.

Telling what a book is isn't so simple after all! About the only thing that a book absolutely has to have in order to be considered a book is a group of pages that can be arranged and held together in a certain order. The pages can be any size, any shape, any number, can be made of any material under the sun. The pages can be arranged in any order that the writer or artist wants to arrange them in, including an order that the reader chooses. The pages can be held together so that they flip, fold, unfold, unroll, slide, pop up, or whatever else makes sense to the person who makes the book. As long as the book has some kind of pages and they are arranged and held together in some way, you have a book!

The important thing to keep in mind is that the way the book works, in addition to the materials it is made of, becomes as much a part of the meaning as the words and pictures in the book. A book of poems about flying that has pop-ups that fly up off the pages may be more interesting than a book of poems about flying that has ordinary flat pages.

Now that you have a better idea of what a book can be, it's easy to understand why more and more people are interested in making their own books. If a book can *be* so many different ways, it can *do* many different things. A book can send information to people who live far away from the writer. It can store and keep information for people to read today or in 80 years. A book can celebrate special occasions, people, places, and friendships. It can even help the writer and the reader think about information and understand it in particular ways.

In reading this book about books you'll make books that do all those things. You'll also learn about remarkable books from around the world and throughout history, books that are rich with information, even though they may not look much like everyday, garden-variety books.

One important note before beginning: The books you'll make will be *your* books, different from anyone else's. The models in this book are just to get you started. The projects will help you think of your own reasons for making books. Once you understand how to make several different kinds of books, use your imagination to invent other kinds of books, books that no one ever dreamed of making until you came along.

HOW TO USE THIS BOOK

This book is designed to help you make books and also to help you think of topics to make books about. The book is divided into four parts: *Books that Carry Messages Across Space and Time; Books that Celebrate and Mark Things; Books that Keep and Save Words, Ideas, and Pictures;* and *Books that Help You Think and Make Sense of Experiences.* Each section has several book projects and book forms to help carry out the projects.

If you already have an idea for a book, decide which big category your idea comes closest to, and then check the projects under that section. Pick out a book form that seems best suited for your idea. If you can't think of an idea right away, do any project that sounds like fun. Each project has general instructions, but also plenty of room for your own ideas. Before starting any of the projects, read the sections on setting up a book center and on tools and materials. Information in those sections is important no matter which projects you decide to do. It's frustrating to be in the middle of a project and discover you don't have a tool you need. If you set up a book center, you'll always have what you need when you need it. The Glossary on page 94 explains many of the terms used in this book. Be sure to look up any words you are not familiar with.

TOOLS AND MATERIALS

SETTING UP A BOOK CENTER

Every book artist needs a place to keep tools and supplies. It's especially nice if you also have a special place to work. An excellent work space can be made out of a table or desk with a nearby lamp, two trash cans, and a couple of shelves made out of bricks and boards for supplies. (See Figure 1.) A simpler work space can be made out of a large cardboard box turned on its side, with a piece of plywood or fiberboard at least 24 by 36 inches (60 by 90 cm) laid across the top. If you don't have a place where you can set up a desk, table, or box, find an old shoe box and a clean plastic trash can to keep your supplies in, and use any clean table or countertop as your work station.

If you take the time to gather all of these materials when you set up your work place, your projects will go smoothly, and you won't have to stop to hunt for materials. However, this is a long list,

and you may not be able to get everything right away. Start with the starred materials; then fill in as you go, gathering or buying whatever you need for each project. That way you will gradually build up a collection of materials.

Materials to Find

You can probably find the following materials around your house:

☆ Newspapers or an old telephone book

☆ Rags

☆ Container for water, such as an empty and clean plastic milk carton (cut down to size) or an aluminum can

☆ Piece of heavy corrugated cardboard at least 24 by 36 inches (60 by 90 cm) to use as a cutting surface

☆ Aluminum pie pan

☆ Roll of paper towels

Waxed paper

Empty paper towel rolls

Scraps of yarn

Old magazines with colored pictures

Materials to Purchase

You will need to buy these materials at an art- or craft-supply store:

☆ Chip board to use for hardback book cover boards (you can use any heavy, smooth cardboard, except for corrugated cardboard, which squashes and dents too easily)

☆ Many different colors, kinds, and sizes of paper (copier paper, wallpaper, wrapping paper, art paper, etc.)

☆ Metal ruler at least 12 inches (30 cm) long, preferably 18 inches (45 cm) long

☆ Several #2 pencils

☆ Rubber eraser

☆ Scissors

Figure 1

Here are some of the tools and materials that will help you make books.

- ☆ Craft knife and extra blades (ask an adult to keep them in a safe place)
- ☆ Awl (sold at hardware stores)
  Hole puncher
- ☆ Several straight sewing needles
- ☆ Good-quality paper glue (or any glue that won't wrinkle paper)
- ☆ Glue brush
- ☆ Waxed or heavy cotton in several colors
  Thread waxer (if you can't find waxed thread, buy this at a sewing-supply store)
- ☆ Small box of large metal paper clips
- ☆ Plastic triangle that has one side with a 90-degree angle
  Materials for illustrating: colored pencils, markers, watercolors, tempera paints
  Paintbrushes
  Stamp pads
  Brayer or roller
  Materials for printing: raw potatoes, plastic or rubber erasers
  Carving tools: ballpoint pen, table knife, linoleum-block carving tools (ask an adult to keep them in a safe place)

Materials to Make
You can make the following equipment:

- ☆ Book press made with two smooth, flat boards, each about 14 by 14 inches (35 by 35 cm), and several bricks or heavy books to use as weights. See Figure 2.
- ☆ Paper storage cabinet made out of a clean, plastic trash can. Roll big pieces of paper into tubes and store them in the trash can.

Figure 2

WRITING YOUR MESSAGE
In most of the books you make you will want to include some form of writing, or *text*. It's important that your writing be easy to read, attractive to look at, and match the contents and style of the book you are making. For example, if you are writing a history of your family, you might want to use handwriting that looks old fashioned. If you are writing a book about racing cars, you might want your printing to look as though it were moving fast!

In order to make the text easy to read, you should first plan how much needs to fit on each page. Book artists make models of their books to use in planning. These models are called *dummies*, but using a dummy is actually a very smart thing to do! To make a dummy, cut and fold paper that is the same size as your book paper. Number the bottom of each page. It isn't necessary to sew the dummy together; just fold the pages into each other or stack them on top of each other. It might help to use paper clips to hold the dummy together. It really doesn't matter how a dummy looks as long as it's a correct model of your book.

Once you have your dummy, you can plan where the text and illustrations will go on each page. You can also see how the pages flow into one another and how the different kinds of folds work. You can also make any changes that seem necessary.

Gather your draft of the text and any drawings or other illustrations you already have. If you will be hand writing your text, write a couple of paragraphs in the size and style you will use in the book in order to see how much space each paragraph or line will take up. If you will be typing your text, type a couple of paragraphs.

Once you have samples of text, figure out how much will fit on each page. Remember to leave room for any illustrations. You can mark right in your dummy. You might simply draw boxes around the spaces where text will be written and then mark your draft "page 2," "page 3," etc., so you will know where to put everything when you write your good copy.

After everything is planned out in your dummy, take your real book pages and very lightly draw horizontal pencil lines where you will be writing. This helps keep your lines straight (or curvy if you want them curvy!) and neat. Check your dummy to see where you should draw lines in the real book. If you will be typing your book, it isn't necessary to draw lines in the good copy.

After guidelines are drawn, carefully letter the text. There are books that show different writing styles, including very fancy ones. If you want to write in a special style, such as the *calligraphy* shown below, look in a book of letter forms or a calligraphy book. When you are finished lettering the book, carefully erase the guidelines.

If you want to type your book, first measure the length of a typical line from the sample paragraphs that you typed. Check your dummy to be sure that *line length* will fit on your pages. If it won't, adjust it until it fits. When you have decided on a good line length, use a computer or a typewriter to type the text. Leave a couple of inches of space between the sections that go on different pages. If you are using a computer, you can make the type any size or style you like.

Once you have typed all of the text, carefully cut out each section. Leave at least 1/4 inch (1 cm) around each section of text. Then put stick-flat glue all over the back of the first section and press it down on the book page where it goes. Press all over carefully to smooth out any air bubbles, and wipe up any extra glue. Continue gluing in all the text sections, being sure to follow the plan in your dummy. When all the gluing is done, slip a piece of waxed paper in between every two pages, and then close the book and press it under a pile of heavy books or in a book press. Pressing the book helps it dry flat.

If you want to decorate the first letter of each paragraph, the letters of the title, or anything else, use watercolors and a fine brush or thin markers after you have written all of the text. Highly decorated initial letters are called *illuminated* letters. There are examples on pages 15, 35, 53, and 71 in this book.

ABCDEFGHIJKLMNOPQ
RSTUVWXYZ 0123456789

abcdefghijklmnopqrstuvwxyz

ILLUSTRATING YOUR IDEAS

Most of the books you will make will have pictures or illustrations. A good illustration adds as much information as the text. Illustrations can show things that are hard to describe in words. For example, the projects in this book all have illustrations in the form of small drawings to help explain the different steps in making the books. Illustrations can also move the reader to feel a certain way, imagine other pictures, and get into the mood of the story.

You may want to make a dummy of the book before you make the real thing; in this way you can see how the text will look and plan the illustrations. Most book artists plan the text and the illustrations more or less at the same time. You can either draw right onto the dummy or make quick sketches to show where drawings or other illustrations should go, and how big they need to be. Some illustrations might spread across more than one page; others might be so small that they can fit inside a single letter! As you are planning the places where you will put illustrations, think about what *kind* of illustrations would go best in your book.

Does your book need careful drawings to help you explain something? Does it need wild, swirly watercolor paintings to create a feeling? How about a few maps, or some photographs of your great uncle Fenwick in the wooden boat he built? Does your book need a border done with potato prints to show all the different shapes of seashells you found at the beach? Different books need different kinds of illustrations. Here are a few techniques to help you get started. Let your imagination run wild as you think of other materials and methods you can use.

Careful Drawings

Some people are able to draw from their imaginations, but most people, even most artists, can't do that very well. However, everyone can learn to draw well what he or she sees. The secret to good

drawing is looking. If you decide you need to draw a person batting a baseball but you "can't" draw people, ask a friend to stand in front of you holding a stick or a baseball bat. Now look carefully. Lightly map out the location of the person's head, arms, legs, feet, and hands. Once everything is drawn lightly in more-or-less stick form, fill out the figure. Turn the stick legs into real legs by looking to see where your friend's leg curves, how long it is, where the knees are located, etc. After you are satisfied with the drawing, give your friend a break, and then darken up the lines and fill in colors.

If you can't find someone to model for you and you need to draw a person, stand in front of a mirror and draw yourself. This is not as easy as drawing another person, but it's definitely possible. If you need to draw a horse and there's no horse around to pose for you, find a photograph of a horse and draw by looking at the photograph. It isn't necessary to trace; just look carefully and draw what you see. Remember, the idea is to draw a believable horse, not to make a copy of the photograph. The more you look and draw, the easier it will become.

Paintings

Another way to illustrate a book is with paintings, such as the small watercolors that illustrate the short features in this book. You can use an inexpensive set of watercolors or watercolor pencils. Use a small or a large paintbrush depending on the size of the pictures you will be painting. You can buy water-soluble graphite pencils in some art-supply stores. These are a great help if you want to do very careful watercolors because you can draw your design first. When you paint over it, the water melts the graphite so that the lines you drew fade into the paint. If you can't find one of these pencils and you want your lines to be precise, use a regular pencil to lightly sketch your design first.

Crayon Resist

Another method of illustration is called *crayon resist*. Begin by drawing a picture with ordinary wax crayons. Then paint over the drawing with watercolors. The wax in the crayons resists the watercolor, so the color fills in only the spaces between the crayon lines and areas, giving a nice background tone.

Collage

You can use magazine pictures or scraps of wrapping paper or other decorated paper to make a *collage*. Ticket stubs, stamps, newspaper pieces, and other thin, flat materials add richness and interest to collages.

Simple Prints

You probably already know how to make potato prints, and they can make interesting borders and designs. Another easy printmaking technique is rubber eraser prints. Find a flat rubber or plastic eraser. Draw a design on the eraser using a roller-ball pen. You will need a simple, bold design to make a good eraser print, so stay away from details or fine lines. Carve away the background from the design using linoleum-block carving tools. Use a stamp pad to print your eraser print.

Try making combinations of several eraser prints to build interesting pictures.

You can also use a plastic foam tray (the kind that grocery stores pack meat or vegetables in). Cut a flat piece from the tray and use a ballpoint pen or a sharp pencil to press a design into the surface. To print, roll tempera paint onto a smooth pie tin with a roller or brayer. Then roll the brayer over the tray. Carefully lay a piece of paper over the inked tray and rub the back of the paper with the back of a spoon. Peel the paper up, and there's your print.

Photographs and Photocopies

On a regular copier, you can make photocopies of black-and-white photographs, enlarging or reducing them to fit the space you have saved for illustrations. For not much money, a copy shop can make a color copy of a color photograph. It's easier to glue a photocopy to the page than a photograph because photographs are thicker than copies.

Books that Carry Messages Across Space and Time

~

A book can send information to people who live far away from the writer. A book can also be a time traveler. Every time you read a book that was written a long time ago, you travel in your imagination back to the time it was written. The projects in this section include a personal time capsule that lets you save a piece of your own history for people (including yourself) to read at some time in the future. There's also a magic carpet that can fly your story to someone else.

Gypsy Wagon

The wandering people of Romania and other parts of Europe traditionally lived in beautiful, brightly colored wooden wagons. Gypsy wagons told of places the people had been and the adventures they had seen. One wagon might be decorated with a carved wooden bird from the Far East; another might sparkle with mirrors and colored glass. Like a gypsy wagon, the book in this project takes you on adventures that change every time you read it!

WHAT YOU NEED

↪ Pack of 3-inch by 5-inch (8 by 13 cm) index cards *— 8 per person?*
↪ Pencils, pens, markers, or other materials for writing text and illustrating the book
↪ 1 piece of heavy-weight decorated cover paper, 10 inches by 40 inches (25 by 100 cm); you can glue smaller sheets together to make one long sheet
↪ Paper clip
↪ Long straightedge, such as a yardstick *rulers*
↪ Triangle
↪ Wooden or cardboard box large enough to hold the cards
↪ Acrylic paints
↪ Paintbrush
↪ Markers

WHAT YOU DO

1. Begin by writing your adventure on the index cards. Since this is a group of possible adventures, you will need to think of many possibilities. At each stage in the book you will ask the reader to make a choice between two possibilities. Your story might be about friends who go searching for treasure, about people long ago who try to find their way out of an enchanted forest, or about people in the future who must deal with living on a distant planet. It could also be a true (or could-be-true) story about your own life and what might have happened if you had made different choices than the ones you already made.

Whatever your adventure is, use the first card to set the scene. Lay it on the floor or on a big empty tabletop. You are going to need a lot of space. Turn the card so that it is longer than it is wide. Label the card "1" in the top left corner. On this first card tell where your story takes place and introduce the main characters. Then give the characters a choice about what they will do next. Here is an example of a first card:

You and your friends John and Lucy are walking in some woods near your house when it begins to rain. This is no ordinary rain but a real downpour. You can hardly see where you are going! Suddenly Lucy points and shouts. Ahead of you in a clearing is a dilapidated old house. **Do you run to the house for shelter, or do you turn around and try to run home?**

2. The choice at the end of the first card leads to two possible actions, and you will write a card for each one. Place two cards on the table under the first card, side by side. See figure 1. Label each of them "2" at the top left corner. Now on each card write what would happen if the characters chose that action. For example, if you and John and Lucy decide to run for home, the first number 2 card might read like this:

You run back down the path, but the rain has changed to hail. You can hardly see, and you are getting pelted by hard little balls! Then John yells, "I think we're lost! I don't remember this place!" **Do you turn back toward the old house, or do you keep trying to find your way home?**

The other number 2 card might read like this:

You aren't exactly happy about it, but you walk toward the empty house. "It's just an abandoned house," you say. But you wonder what it's doing in the middle of the woods. The door creaks as it swings open into darkness. **Do you go inside, or do you huddle outside on the porch trying to keep dry?**

3. You now have three cards, and each of the number 2 cards asks a question that leads to two more cards. So lay out two cards under each number 2 card. You will write four possible actions for the number 3 cards. After each action, write a choice, as you did on the number 1 and 2 cards.

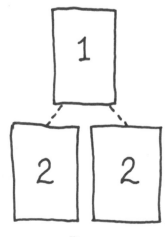

Figure 1

4. Continue your adventures until you reach their endings. They don't all have to end at the same time. For example, one adventure might end after only five choices. The others can keep on going. See Figure 2 to see what your cards might look like when they are all written. Notice that only two go on to level six, and that many end at level four and five. Be sure to label each card with the number that tells its level. That's important so you can keep the choices in order.

5. To make a case to display each adventure, you'll need that long piece of decorated paper. Use the paper clip and straightedge to *score* a line 2 inches (5 cm) up from the bottom and all the way across, lengthwise. See Figure 3. To score, press hard enough to make a mark with a rounded edge of the paper clip. Scoring makes folding easier.

6. Score another line 2 inches (5 cm) down from the top and all the way across the other long side. See Figure 4.

7. Fold the paper in along the two scored lines. See Figure 5.

8. Use the triangle and paper clip to score nine vertical, or up and down, lines 4 inches (10 cm) apart all along the width of the folded paper. The scored lines should start at the top fold and end at the bottom fold. If you line up the triangle along the straight folded edge, your vertical lines should go straight up and down. See Figure 6.

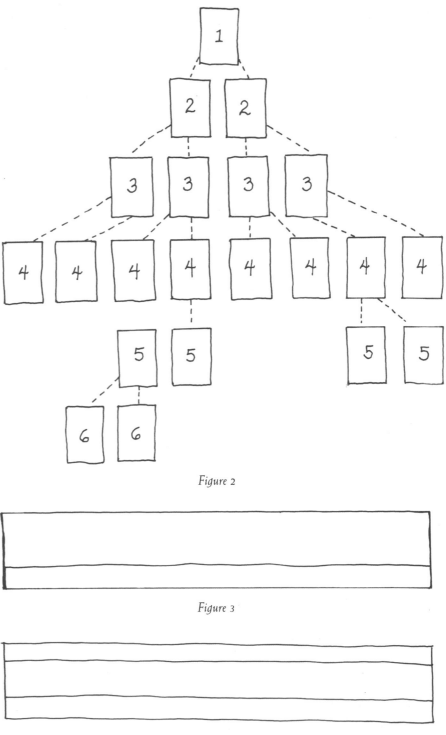

Figure 2

Figure 3

Figure 4

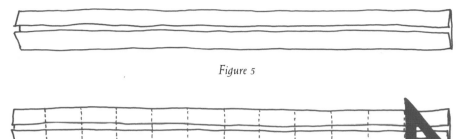

Figure 5

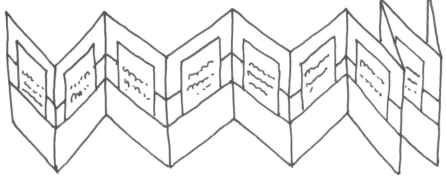

Figure 6

9. Fold along the scored lines in accordion fashion to create a cover or case with many little pockets. See Figure 7.

10. Place each chosen card in its pocket next to the one that comes before it. You can fold up the case or keep it open on a shelf for other people to read. To change the adventure, simply take the cards out of the pockets, arrange all the cards in order of their numbers, and choose another adventure!

11. Use acrylic paints or markers to decorate the box in which you will store all the cards and the case.

Figure 7

Time Capsule

Have you ever discovered a box of old letters or faded photographs in the attic? When you looked at the pictures or read the words did you feel as though you were visiting another time period? Finding treasures like these is like finding a time capsule—a visitor from another period of history.

Some time capsules are accidental ones, like a box of dusty souvenirs from a long-ago vacation. But you can also make a time capsule by storing in a special book pictures and writings that show what your time period is like. Then you write on the book when the time capsule is to be opened. All time capsules carry with them the words, images, ideas, songs, fashions, fads, and personalities of the people who made them.

You can make a time capsule for yourself to be opened later in your lifetime, or you can make one for other people to open many, many years from now. The time capsule in this project is a book that is designed to hide its contents until the pages are cut open. At that exact moment, the time capsule becomes a book about the past!

WHAT YOU NEED

- 6 to 8 sheets of copier or construction paper, 8½ inches by 11 inches (22 by 28 cm)
- Glue stick
- Ruler
- Large paper clips
- Pen or pencil for writing text
- Materials for illustrating the time capsule
- Photographs, picture postcards, newspaper articles, paper souvenirs, such as theater tickets
- Piece of scrap cardboard
- Awl
- Large-eyed sewing needle
- 1 piece of string or heavy thread, 4 feet (1.2 m) long

WHAT YOU DO

1. Glue together the short sides of at least six pieces of paper. For a longer book, glue more pieces together. See Figure 1.

2. Use the ruler and paper clip to score lines every 6 inches (15 cm) along the entire length of the long strip. Each score line marks the edges of a page. Scoring will make the strip easier to fold into its pages, so press hard and score a few times to make each fold line. See Figure 2. Now fold back and forth, accordion style, until all the pages are folded. Cut off any leftover paper.

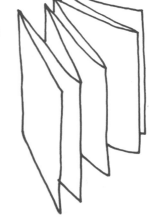

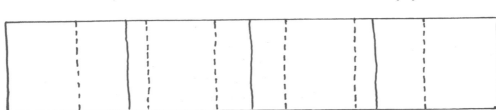

Figure 1

Figure 2

3. Open out the accordion. Leave the first and last pages blank; they will become the two covers of the book. On each of the other pages, write, draw, or glue the contents of your time capsule. Whatever you put in the time capsule should help give a good picture of you and your life at this time. What will help tell this story? Be sure to keep a blank margin 1½ inches (4 cm) in from each edge. Write only on one side of the strip of paper.

4. When all your pages are filled (except for the first and last), fold up the accordion.

What you are holding looks like a book, and if you turn the pages, you can see what you have written.

5. Now, with the book closed, turn it over, (turn it from side to side, not top to bottom, because you don't want the writing to be upside down). Put a couple of

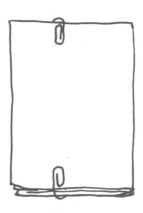

Figure 3

large paper clips along the left edge of the book to hold everything together while you sew. See Figure 3 on page 21.

6. Cover your work surface with the piece of cardboard to protect it. Use the awl to poke several holes about 1 inch (2.5 cm) apart, beginning 1 inch (2.5 cm) from the top and bottom edges and ½ inch (1.5 cm) in from the spine of the book. You will have to screw the awl back and forth to make it go through all the thicknesses of paper. See Figure 4.

7. Turn the book over while it's still clipped together and widen the holes from the back.

8. Thread the needle and insert it into the first hole at either end. Pull the thread until a tail 1 foot (30 cm) long is left. Hold that tail in place with a paper clip while you sew. Wrap the thread around the outside of the book and go back into the same hole. Pull tight. See Figure 5.

9. Poke the needle into the next hole down and pull the thread tight. Again, wrap the thread around the outside of the book and go back into the same hole. Then insert the needle into the next hole. Repeat until you have gone into each of the holes.

10. After you have poked the needle back into the bottom hole (after wrapping the thread around the outside of the book), simply go in and out of each hole until you reach the top of the book. Don't wrap the thread around the outside of the book this time. As you sew your way up to the top hole, you will be filling in the spaces between holes where there was no thread. See Figure 6. When

you get to the top, tie the end of the thread to the tail that you clipped under the paper clip.

11. Remove the paper clips. Cut the tails off evenly, and either thread a bead through one thread, braid the tails, fray them, or tie them together. Or you can make bows with the tails, or cut them off short. This kind of binding is called a *stab binding.*

12. Make a title for your time capsule and write it on the cover.

13. Open the book to the first page, which will be blank because the writing and pictures are all on the inside. This first page is the place to write your name and today's date, as well as directions telling when and how to open the time capsule. (To open the time capsule, slide a dinner knife or scissors inside each fold, and slit the folded edge.)

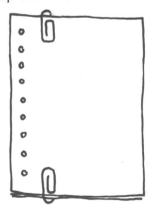

Figure 4

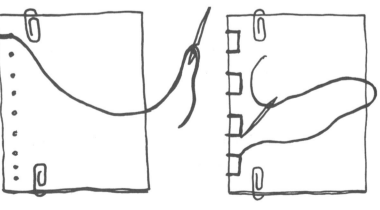

Figure 5

Figure 6

A 3300-Year-Old Time Capsule

What do a prehistoric sailing ship, a jar full of pomegranates, and a tiny wooden book have in common? It's a strange tale, and the strangest part is that it's true!

The story begins in what historians call the Late Bronze Age—around 3300 years ago. A large sailing ship heavily loaded with trade goods such as melons, pomegranates, olives, oils, ivory, glass ingots, tin, and copper was battling a storm in the Mediterranean Sea. As the ship rounded the southern coast of Turkey, the wild winds blasted even stronger, and the ship broke in half and sank in 150 feet of water.

Now fast forward to the 1980s, when a team of nautical archaeologists from Texas A & M University, headed by underwater explorer and archaeologist George Bass, was excavating that very shipwreck, the oldest ever discovered. Late Bronze Age ships like this one carried cargo in large clay pots. Some of these giant pots, called *pithos*, were big enough for you and a friend to climb inside of together. One day the archaeologists were carefully sifting the contents of a pithos that had been filled with fresh red pomegranates. (They were able to identify the pomegranates because of seeds and other parts of the fruits that had survived more than 3000 years buried at sea!) Someone discovered some fragments of wood with traces of what looked like an ivory hinge still attached. Careful piecing together of these puzzle pieces revealed that they were the remains of a small wooden book called a *diptych*, consisting of two wooden leaves or pages joined by a hinge. This particular diptych was about 4 inches tall (10 cm) and had a three-part ivory hinge. The two pages were made of hard, close-grained boxwood, and their inner surfaces had been hollowed out. Melted wax had been poured onto the scooped out surfaces. People wrote in these books by scratching into the wax with a pencil-like tool called a *stylus*.

The archaeologists think that perhaps this diptych had been used as a kind of receipt, telling the number and price of the pomegranates. We know for certain that this tiny book was in the pithos of pomegranates when the ship went down that day 34 centuries ago. This fact makes the little diptych from the pomegranate pithos the oldest book of its kind ever found.

Magic Carpet

Books are magic carpets that fly readers to faraway places and long ago times.
This book not only acts like a magic carpet, but it looks like one, too. And when
you want to pack it away, it folds up into its own carrying case.

WHAT YOU NEED

- ✦ 1 large sheet of white or light-colored paper, 18 inches by 24 inches (45 by 60 cm); you can glue several sheets of copier paper edge to edge to make one big sheet
- ✦ Ruler
- ✦ Pencil or pen
- ✦ Materials to illustrate the story and make a border for the carpet, such as markers, crayons, rubber stamps, or carved potatoes
- ✦ Sheet of heavy paper or light cardboard, about 10 inches by 20 inches (25 by 50 cm)
- ✦ Scissors
- ✦ Large paper clip
- ✦ Good-quality paper glue
- ✦ Glue brush

WHAT YOU DO

1. To create pages from the one large sheet of paper, use the ruler to make a mark every 6 inches (15 cm) along the short sides, and every 8 inches (20 cm) along the long sides. See Figure 1.

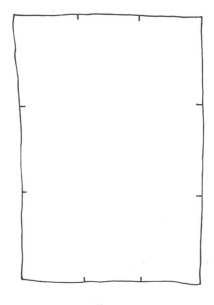

Figure 1

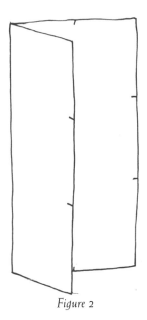

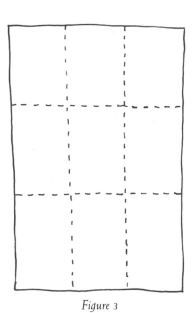

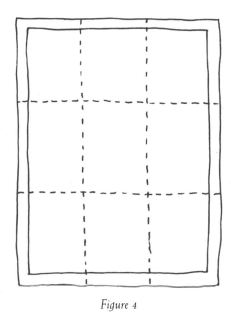

| Figure 2 | Figure 3 | Figure 4 |

2. Now fold a line that goes from the first 6-inch (15 cm) mark on one short side to the first 6-inch (15 cm) mark on the other short side. See Figure 2.

3. Fold lines that join all the other side marks. You should have folds along all the dotted lines, as shown in Figure 3.

4. Unfold the paper. You should see nine boxes made by the folded lines. Each of these boxes is a page in your book.

5. Book artists need to plan their books, and that is what you will do next. Think of the story that you want to tell in this book. It would be a good idea to write a draft of the story. Decide if you want any pages to be all or part illustration. You might want to make a border that goes all around the outside of the big sheet of paper and helps tell your story by showing designs or printed shapes that go with the story. If you want a border, draw a light pencil line 1 to 1½ inches (2.5 to 4 cm) inside the outside edge all around the large sheet. See Figure 4.

6. After your draft is written and you've decided on a design or plan for the illustrations as well as the written part (text), divide the draft copy of the story up with marks to show which part of it goes on each of the text pages.

7. Now put the text in your book using one of the methods described on pages 10 and 11. Illustrate the book with one of the methods described on pages 12 and 13.

8. After the magic carpet is finished, fold it up. Lay the sheet of heavy paper that you will use for the case on the table with the 20-inch edges (50 cm) at the top and the bottom. Lay the folded book on one edge of the piece of heavy paper, positioned so that a 6-inch (15 cm) edge of the book is lined up on a 10-inch (25 cm) edge of the heavy paper. Push the book 1 inch (2.5 cm) toward the center of the heavy paper and centered between the top and bottom edges of the heavy paper. See Figure 5.

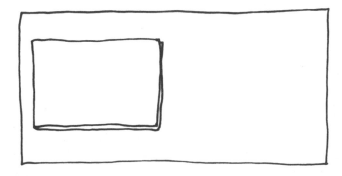

Figure 5

9. Draw a light pencil line around the outside of the folded book. Make this line slightly larger than the book so the case won't be too tight. Then move the book so that one 6-inch (15 cm) edge touches the line that you drew on the right side. See Figure 6.

10. Draw a light pencil line around the outside of the folded book as you did before, leaving a little extra space so the case is not too tight. You should now have two pencil outlines of the book, touching each other along one 6-inch (15 cm) side.

11. Draw a 1-inch-wide (2.5 cm) tab at both 6-inch (15 cm) ends, and a 1-inch (2.5 cm) tab at two of the 8-inch (20 cm) sides. See Figure 7.

12. Cut out the heavy paper along the lines you have drawn. See Figure 8.

13. Use a large paper clip and a ruler to score lines along all the remaining pencil lines. Now fold the case along all the scored lines.

14. Put glue on the two short tabs, and fold them over to strengthen the edges of the case. See Figure 9.

15. Fold the case in half. Put glue on the two remaining tabs and press them over onto the outside of the case to hold it closed. See Figure 10.

16. Let the glue dry; then decorate the cover of the case. Slip the folded carpet into its case.

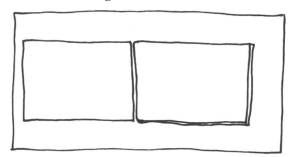

Figure 6

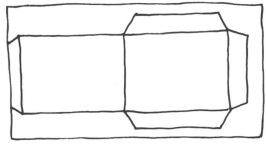

Figure 7

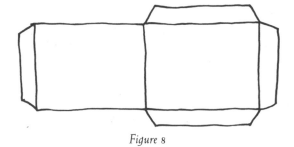

Figure 8

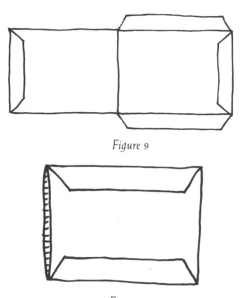

Figure 9

Figure 10

Tool Kit

Let's say you're an expert on snakes. You can identify what kind they are, and you know their individual habits, diets, and how to build environments in which they can live happily ever after. When a snake slithers into your neighbors' basement, guess who they call? You—the Snake Charmer! In fact, people so often ask your advice about snakes that you sometimes think about writing a book. Then you could simply hand it out when friends say to you, "Tell me how to take care of a snake!"

The how-to book in this project is just what you need. It's like a tool kit; the facts are the tools. You can write a how-to book about any subject you know a lot about—babysitting, gardening, skateboarding, pets, or magic tricks. And here's a little magic: you may think you're an expert now, but you're going to know even more when you finish writing your book!

WHAT YOU NEED

- ➴ White copier paper, 8½ inches by 11 inches (22 by 28 cm); 25 pieces make a good sized book, but you can make yours longer or shorter
- ➴ Pencil or pen for writing text
- ➴ Materials for illustrating book
- ➴ 2 pieces of cover cardboard, each 8½ inches by 6 inches (22 by 15 cm)
- ➴ Decorative paper to cover the cardboard (or plain paper, if you want to draw your own decorations)
- ➴ Scissors
- ➴ Good-quality paper glue
- ➴ Glue brush
- ➴ 1 piece of scrap cardboard
- ➴ Awl
- ➴ Curved sewing needle
- ➴ 1 piece of waxed linen or cotton thread, 6 feet (1.9 m) long

WHAT YOU DO

1. Fold the text pages in half so that each one measures 8½ by 5½ inches (22 by 14 cm). Slip the pages inside each other in groups of five, which will give you five groups, called *signatures*. (This division works well if you use 25 sheets; if you use more or fewer sheets, just divide them into signatures of five.)

2. Write your text and draw the pictures. If you need more pages, add them in signatures of five. If you don't need all 25 sheets, take away one signature. It's okay to have some blank pages at the back of a how-to book so that the reader can take notes.

3. To make the front cover, place a piece of cardboard on top of a piece of decorative paper. Draw around the cardboard to make glue tabs, as shown in Figure 1. Be sure to leave a small space, as thick as the cover board thickness, at points A, B, C, and D.

4. Cut out the paper along the lines you have drawn. Brush glue all over the undecorated side of the paper.

5. Carefully lay the cover board between points A, B, C, and D, and fold the flaps up as shown in Figure 2. Smooth and press the paper all over to make sure it sticks everywhere, paying special attention to the corners.

6. Cut a piece of decorated paper slightly smaller than the cover board. Put glue all over the undecorated side and then press it down over the cover flaps, as shown in Figure 3. To make the back cover, repeat steps 3, 4, 5, and 6.

7. Hold the two covers together the way they will be when the book is finished. Cover your work surface with the scrap cardboard. Use the awl to poke a row of holes around 1 inch (2.5 cm) apart in both covers at the same time along their left edges, as shown in Figure 4. You may want to ask an adult to help you. The holes need to be at least ½ inch (1.5 cm) in from the edge so they don't tear. Twist the awl in a screwlike motion and press straight down. You probably won't be able to poke the holes in the bottom cover all the way through; that's okay, as long as they are at least

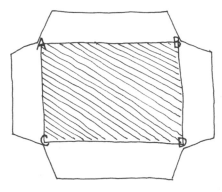

Figure 1

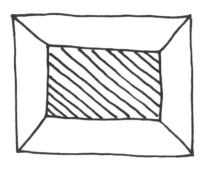

Figure 2

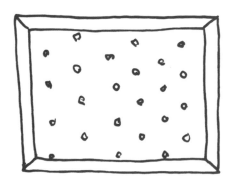

Figure 3

marked. Take the front cover away and finish making the holes in the bottom cover.

8. Gather all the signatures together and place them between the covers, just as they will be when the book is finished. Holding the book tightly closed on a tabletop, use a pencil to draw a line down from signature fold to signature fold below each of the cover holes. These pencil marks on the outside of the folds of each signature will tell you where to poke the holes in the signatures, so be sure each one gets all of its marks. See Figure 5.

9. Open out each signature and use the awl to make holes where you made pencil marks (which should be on the *outside* fold of each signature).

10. Thread the curved needle and tie a knot in one end of the thread.

11. Pick up either cover and the first signature next to that cover. Put the needle into the first hole from either end of the signature from the *inside*. Pull the thread through. Reach around the cover with the needle and insert it into the first hole of the cover from the *outside*. Pull the thread through between the cover and the first signature, being sure to pull in the same direction as the *spine* or edge of the book, and not straight up. Pulling straight up will tear the paper, so always pull parallel to the spine. Poke the needle back into the first hole of the signature from the *outside*. Now, on the *inside* of the signature, move up to the next hole, and repeat step 11.

12. Repeat step 11 until all the cover holes are sewn and the cover is joined to the first signature. Stop when you come to the last cover hole.

Figure 4

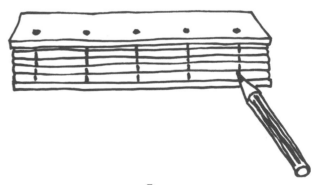

Figure 5

13. On the last cover hole, don't go back into the last hole of the first signature. Instead, pick up the second signature and go into the first hole of it from the *outside*. See Figure 6.

14. Now you are on the *inside* of the second signature. Insert the needle into the second hole and pull the thread to the *outside*. On the *outside*, use the curve of the needle to scoop the little piece of thread that is between the cover and the first signature. Then put the needle back into the second hole of the second signature from the *outside*. The little scoop stitch is what holds the second signature to the first signature. Repeat step 14 until all the holes in the second signature are sewn.

15. Repeat steps 13 and 14 to sew all the rest of the signatures. *Always be sure to scoop the thread that is between the signature you are sewing and the one you just finished sewing.* Don't go back and scoop the thread between the cover and the first signature once you have finished the second signature or the spine of the book will curl in too tightly.

16. Repeat step 11 to sew on the back cover. When you finish the last hole, tie off the thread on the *inside* of the signature. See Figure 7. This type of binding is called *Coptic binding* and is very old.

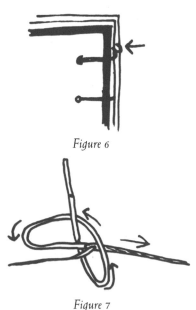

Figure 6

Figure 7

PAGES OF SILK, COVERS OF IVORY

We're used to seeing books made of paper, cardboard, and even cloth. Nowadays it's easy to find a book with pop-ups and even a book that plays music when you open it or that smells like fresh oranges or chocolate when you scratch the pictures. But most of these books are made in the form called a *codex*—groups of pages bound together between covers. So when book artists today search for new forms and materials for their books, they are often guided by books from the past and from many different parts of the

world where books have been made in amazing forms.

In Southeast Asia, long-ago books were made of gold writing inlaid in thin sheets of ivory. The ivory "pages" were not bound but were kept stacked in small ivory or wooden boxes like the one on the facing page.

Palm leaves have been used for books by people living in India and Southeast Asia. A few from the 18th and 19th centuries still survive. The palm leaves were cut into slats like modern venetian blind slats and strung together with a strip of wood at each end of the stack for covers. Words were scratched into the surface of the leaves with a stylus, and then the scratches were filled with black pigment, such as charred wood, so they would show up better. So many books were made of different kinds of leaves that the word "leaf" began to be used to mean a page, and we still call pages "leaves."

People in Sumatra wrote on folds of the inner bark of trees and then bound their books between heavy wooden boards. Sumatran medicine men made private notebooks in this way that they called *pustahas*. The bark pages were folded back and forth accordion style, and the book was often tied closed with a piece of cord like the one drawn on page 30.

The Japanese have made accordion-folded books for centuries. Originally, their books were made by gluing

sheets of paper together to form long strips of paper, which were then rolled into scrolls. Sometimes scrolls were made of silk. These books were called *kansuban*, which means "rolled book." The problem with scrolls is that it's hard to find something in the middle of the book, and so around the year 800 other styles of books began to be developed in both China and Japan. The accordion-fold book was made by folding the long piece of paper back and forth and then attaching a cover to each end. When a single cover was wrapped around the book and attached to both ends, the book was called a flutter book (*sempuyo*) because the accordion-folded pages were not attached at the spine of the book but could flutter forward easily.

Around 1100 B.C., the Assyrian people made a kind of book by inscribing pages of writing on clay tablets that formed the sides of octagonal cylinders. The reader turned the cylinder as he or she finished reading each "page."

The Romans wrote on waxed writing tablets. Some of their notebooks consisted of as many as nine pages bound together with leather laces. Even though these books were clumsy to use and carry, the waxed surfaces could be smoothed out and written on again and again.

Even the simple codex has been changed by people over time. In the 15th century in France, heart-shaped books were all the rage. One beautifully illustrated book of love songs covered in red velvet formed the shape of a single heart when it was closed and the shape of two hearts joined together when it was opened.

Traveling Museum

Your teacher has asked you to write a report on dinosaurs. As you flip through one of the books you found in the library, you remember the visit you made to a famous museum last summer. Being in the museum made you feel like you were living in another time and place. There was a dinosaur as tall as a three-story building looming in the center of the room. Lining the walls were models of the dinosaur's habitat. Carefully lettered signs explained what the dinosaur ate, how it defended itself, and what caused it to become extinct. You could even press a button and listen to a recording of dinosaurlike sounds. If only you could make your report as exciting as that museum's exhibit!

This book can help you do just that. It unfolds in unexpected ways, giving you places to glue maps and big pictures or to reveal extra-long time lines. It's easy to make, but looks complicated. You can change it to suit the material you want to put in your report. This kind of folded paper is called origami.

WHAT YOU NEED

- ✎ 1 large sheet of paper, at least 17 inches by 22 inches (43 by 55 cm)
- ✎ Scissors
- ✎ Materials to write and illustrate the report
- ✎ Good-quality paper glue
- ✎ Glue brush

WHAT YOU DO

1. Fold the piece of paper in half the long way. See Figure 1.

2. Then fold the long strip in half, and in half again. See Figure 2.

3. Unfold the sheet of paper. You should have creases that look like Figure 3.

4. Make a cut from point A to point B, as shown in Figure 4.

5. There are a couple of different ways that you can fold the book. One way is to fold section 1 onto section 2, onto section 3, onto section 4, back and forth like an accordion. Then fold everything under section 5 (see Figure 5). Continue folding like an accordion until every section is folded. This method of folding gives you a double-wide page where sections 4 and 5 touch each other.

6. Experiment with different ways of folding and displaying this book. You can attach small signatures in some of the folds, similar to the hypertext in the Treasure Chest on page 54. You can also add other sheets of paper that fold out from the pages.

7. Write and illustrate your report in such a way that as you unfold the book, each section is like a part of a museum exhibit. When you unfold the whole book at once, it will be like a model of a large exhibit.

Figure 1

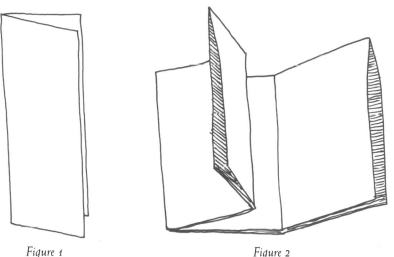

Figure 2

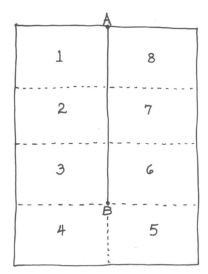

Figure 3

Figure 4

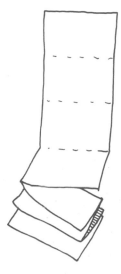

Figure 5

No Talking, No Eating, and No Checking Out the Books, Either!

If you think the rules in your school library are strict (all those due dates, overdue fines, and no talking or snacking), imagine how you would have felt in the medieval library at Hereford Cathedral in England. In this library the books were actually chained to the shelves! If you wanted to read one of them, the librarian had to help you lift the book, chain and all, down to a kind of table below the shelf. There you could sit (without talking or eating!) on a wooden bench that looked like a church pew and browse through the book. But you absolutely could not check it out or even carry it across the room. In those days, books were such rare and precious objects that in many libraries they were chained up so they wouldn't be stolen.

If you think it's hard to find a book on a certain topic in your school library, imagine trying to find a particular book in the ancient Egyptian library in the city of Alexandria. This library had about 400,000 papyrus scrolls and no cataloging system until years after it opened! In fact, finding a particular scroll was such a horrendous job that the librarians were driven to invent the first library cataloging system.

And if you sometimes get tired of lugging your books back and forth to the library, be glad they aren't made of clay tablets, as were the books of the ancient Babylonians. The very first libraries that we know of were giant storehouses in Babylonia and Egypt full of clay tablets and papyrus scrolls containing written records.

BOOKS THAT CELEBRATE AND MARK THINGS

Everyone loves holidays, special events, or remarkable places. A book can be a great way to celebrate your favorite people, places, and occasions. Was your tenth birthday party the best yet? Do you want to help your sister remember and appreciate her first day of kindergarten? If you make a book about these special times, you can celebrate over and over again each time you look at your book! Projects in this section include making a scroll to mark a special process, and an exciting way to dive deep into a special place and celebrate its beauty, history, and people.

Deep Map

A man named William Least Heat Moon wrote a book called Prairyerth *(1991) that he called a deep map. It told many stories and provided a great deal of information about a very small place. Instead of being a map that spread far and wide, it was a map that seemed to go deep into time and also into the earth.*

A regular map shows roads, boundaries, cities and towns, natural features, such as rivers, lakes, and mountains, and sometimes even buildings, parks, and special attractions. A deep map goes beneath the surface and tells about what used to be there, about the plants and animals that live in a place, about the people who live there now and who used to live there, about the feel, sounds, and smells of a place. A deep map can be as deep as you want it to be. You might want to tell a lot about the very earliest people who lived in a place, or you might want to tell where the squirrels that live there now like to congregate.

WHAT YOU NEED

- Paper for pages; these can be any size you want. It's a good idea to collect information for your deep map before you start making it. That way you'll have an idea how many pages you need and what sizes they need to be. For example, you might want some extra long pages that can be folded into the book for time lines. All the pages in the book should be the same height, even if some are longer than others.
- Pencil, pen, and other drawing materials
- 1 piece of heavy paper for the cover; it should be at least two and a half times as wide as the text pages, and the same height as the text pages
- Ruler
- Scissors
- Small paper clip
- Strong paper clamp
- Rubber band, 2 to 3 inches (5 to 7.5 cm) long
- Stick that you found in the place that the book is about, 3 inches (7.5 cm) long, and about as thick as a pencil
- Awl

WHAT YOU DO

1. The first thing to do is collect information about the place you want to deep map. What does the land look like today? What can you find out about the way the land used to look? Go to the public library and ask for copies of any maps that include this place. Old maps are especially interesting. Look in old city directories to see who used to live and work in the place years ago. Look in the current directory to see who lives and works there now.

Take a walk in the place. What plants grow there? What animals live there? Can you find any animal homes? What kinds of houses and other buildings are there? Talk to the people who live and work there. What can you learn from their stories about the place? What are the special sounds, songs, smells, foods, holidays of this place? Are there any cemeteries? What can you learn about who used to live there? Make drawings and maps of your own, as well as take notes and photographs.

2. When you have lots of information about the place, think about how you want to put it in the book. Decide how big the pages need to be. What will it take to give a good, deep picture of this special place? Do you need any pages that are extra long and will fold out? Do you need any that have special shapes? Decide which pictures, photographs, or drawings you would like to include. Write up the stories you want to tell. Make time lines, charts, and diagrams to give other information.

3. Make a dummy of your book for planning both the text and the illustrations. (See page 10 on planning a book.) Your dummy will tell you how big your pages need to be. Gather all the blank sheets of paper together.

4. Write and draw everything on every page. Be sure to leave a space at least 1½ inches (4 cm) wide at the left side of each paper because that is where the binding will be. Assemble all the sheets of paper in the order you want them to be in. Fold in any extra long sheets. Be sure to include a title page and maybe a blank page at the beginning and at the end of the book.

5. Make a cover for the book out of the heavy paper. To do so, place the stack of pages in one corner of the paper. Place the ruler across the top. See Figure 1.

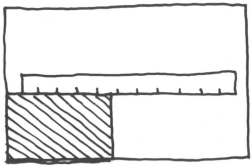

Figure 1

6. Remove the stack of pages, but don't move the ruler. Draw a line along the bottom edge of the ruler. Cut the paper along that line.

7. Place the stack of pages at one end of the piece of cover paper that you have just cut. See Figure 2. Use the small paper clip to score a line on the cover paper along the side of the stack of paper. Remove the stack of paper, and use the ruler and paper clip to score another line as far away from the first one as the book is thick. See Figure 3.

8. Lay the stack of pages on the cover paper so that its left edge lines up with the second scored line (see Figure 4). Score along the right edge of the stack. Remove the stack and cut along the line you've just scored. Fold the cover along the other two scored lines as shown in Figure 5. Slip the pages into the cover. See Figure 6.

9. Tap the book on a tabletop so that the pages all line up. Clip the book with the large paper clamp along the right edge to hold the pages in place while you bind it. See Figure 7.

10. Use the awl to poke a hole through the covers and all the pages at one time, as shown in Figure 8. Keep the awl straight up and down while pressing hard and screwing it back and forth. Try poking through from one end, then turning the book over and widening out the hole from the other side. Poke this hole around ½ inch (1.5 cm) down from the top edge and ½ inch (1.5 cm) from the spine. Poke a second hole ½ inch (1.5 cm) up from the bottom and ½ inch in (1.5 cm) from the spine.

11. Unbend the small paper clip; then squeeze a narrow bend or hook in one end. This hook will help you thread the rubber band through the holes. With the front cover facing you, slip the hook through one of the holes. Put the rubber band on the hook, and pull the hook and rubber band about ½ inch (1.5 cm) through the hole. See Figure 9.

12. Slip one end of the stick through this loop of the rubber band. Now stick the hook through the other hole, and hook the other end of the rubber band. Pull this end through the hole, and slip this loop onto the other end of the stick. See Figure 10. Decorate the cover to finish your deep map.

Figure 2

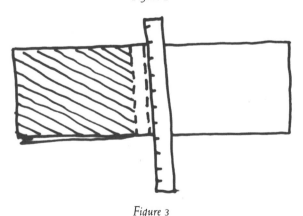

Figure 3

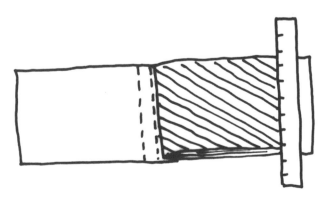

Figure 4

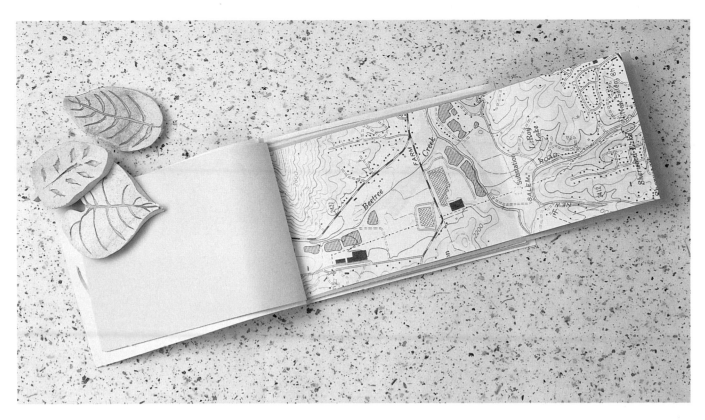

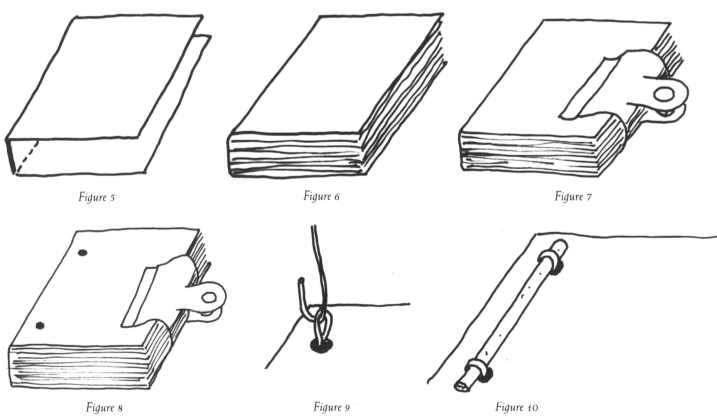

Figure 5

Figure 6

Figure 7

Figure 8

Figure 9

Figure 10

Movie

The book in this project combines a very old form of communicating information—a scroll—with a newer approach—a movie. Scrolls have been around since ancient times, and they are still a nice way to unroll a story or tell about a process.

WHAT YOU NEED

- Cardboard box, about 4 inches by 4 inches by 8 inches (10 by 10 by 20 cm)
- 2 cardboard rolls from paper towels or wrapping paper
- Pencil
- Craft knife
- Ruler
- Scissors
- Several sheets of white or light-colored copier paper
- Good-quality paper glue
- Glue brush
- Materials for writing text and illustrating the book
- 1 sheet of self-adhesive shelf paper, 3 feet (.9 m) long
- Acrylic paint
- Paintbrush

WHAT YOU DO

1. Stand the cardboard box on a table so that the bottom faces you. The bottom will become the front of the movie screen. You'll need holes in the box to slip the rollers into, so trace around each roller as shown in Figure 1. Be sure the rollers are ½ inch (1.5 cm) in from the front and side edges of the box.

2. Ask an adult to help you cut out the circles you have traced. Then, slip the cardboard rollers into the holes. Reach into the box and trace around the rollers where they touch the other side of the box. See Figure 2. Take the rollers out of the box. Ask an adult to help you cut out these two circles.

3. Use the ruler to help you draw a rectangle for the movie screen. This rectangle should be the size that you want your "pages" to be. After you've drawn the rectangle, ask an adult to help you cut it out. See Figure 3.

4. Measure the height of the screen. Cut the copier paper into long strips that are the same height as the screen, plus 1 inch (2.5 cm). Glue the strips together to make one long strip as long as you need. See Figure 4.

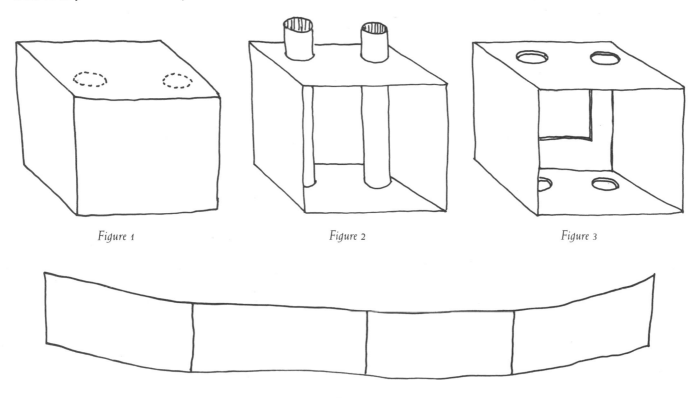

Figure 1   Figure 2   Figure 3

Figure 4

5. Begin writing and drawing 5 inches (13 cm) in from the left end of the scroll. Be sure to make each page as wide as the rectangle of your screen. It might help to draw borders the size of the screen around each page. See Figure 5. Leave 5 inches (13 cm) blank at the end of the scroll.

6. Cover the outside front, top, and sides of the box with self-adhesive shelf paper. Push the two rollers into their holes. Leave about 1 inch (2.5 cm) sticking out at the top and bottom of each roller. See Figure 6.

7. Roll up the scroll so that the text and illustrations face outward. Reach into the back of the box and tape or glue the left-hand edge of the scroll to the roller that is on the right when you look at the box from the back. See Figure 7.

8. From the back, turn the roller clockwise (toward the right) to wrap the entire scroll around the roller. Leave about 10 inches (25 cm) unrolled.

9. Pull the loose end of the scroll over the front of the other roller. Turn the first roller to take up more slack if you need to. Tape or glue the end of the scroll to the second roller. See Figure 8.

10. Turn the box around. Adjust the position of the scroll by pushing the rollers up or down. Practice rolling the story across the screen.

11. Paint the ends of the rollers with acrylic paint. Let the show begin!

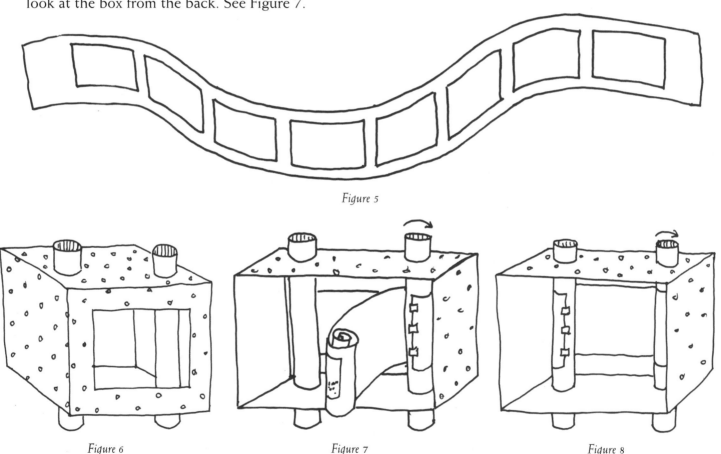

Figure 5

Figure 6   Figure 7   Figure 8

THE DEAD SEA SCROLLS

One day in 1949, a Bedouin shepherd who lived near Kumran by the Dead Sea in the Middle East was looking for a lost sheep. He was searching among some rocks when he discovered a small cave. The shepherd forgot all about his sheep, when, to his amazement, he found several large clay jars hidden inside the cave.

He pulled one of the jars from the cave and found that it was sealed with a lid. He pried the lid off and saw some packages inside. They were wrapped in what looked to him like ancient cloth, smeared with a black, tarlike substance. The shepherd realized that he had found something that might be very old and valuable, so he went to get help and advice.

The jars were brought to a laboratory in a museum where they were carefully unpacked. The packages inside turned out to be parchment scrolls wrapped in linen cloth and sealed with bitumen, a tarlike material which was used in ancient times to seal and protect objects. The scrolls were unrolled with great care. Although they were brittle with age, scientists were able to decipher them, determine their age, and who wrote them.

The writing on the scrolls was Hebrew and Aramaic, and the texts were scriptures that went with the Bible, as well as comments on Bible texts. The scrolls were written between 1,900 and 2,000 years ago by a group of people called the Essenes.

The *Dead Sea Scrolls*, as we call them, are a true time capsule, carrying their messages from ancient times to modern days, waiting all those centuries in their hiding place. No one knows why they were buried, but their careful wrapping and hiding place kept them safe from harm.

Journal Companion

If you're a writer, artist, inventor, or someone who's always thinking of good ideas and wanting to remember them, you need a journal on hand at all times. You never know when you'll get an idea or see something you want to sketch or hear something you want to write down. This journal is designed to fit in a small bag that ties to your belt. This type of book-in-a-bag is called a polaire.

WHAT YOU NEED

- 1 piece of corrugated cardboard (single thickness), 5 inches by 11 inches (13 by 28 cm)
- 10 to 12 sheets of drawing or writing paper, each 4½ inches by 10 inches (11 by 25 cm)
- Awl
- 1 piece of heavy waxed thread, 2 feet (60 cm) long
- Sewing needle
- Scissors
- Old sock that does NOT have a hole in its toe
- 1 piece of rope or twine, 2 feet (60 cm) long
- Short pencil or pen

WHAT YOU DO

1. Turn the corrugated cardboard so that one of its short ends faces you. Roll up the cardboard, beginning at the 5 inch (13 cm) end that is nearest you. As it rolls, the cardboard will bend between the ribs. Keep rolling until you have a fat roll of cardboard 5 inches (13 cm) tall. See Figure 1. (Instead of rolling the whole thing from one end, it may be easier to roll first from one end and then from the other.)

2. Unroll the cardboard. It will stay bent and curly. Fold it in half.

3. Make a signature by folding all the sheets of paper in half and slip them inside the cardboard cover. Unfold the cover, keeping the pages facing up.

4. Ask an adult to help you use the awl to poke three holes through the cardboard and all the sheets of paper at once, about 1 inch (2.5 cm) apart, in the fold of the book. Be careful not to move the pages; the holes must stay lined up. Gently wiggle the awl to enlarge the holes until they are big enough for the sewing needle to fit through. See Figure 2.

5. Thread the needle with the heavy thread but do not tie a knot.

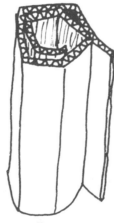

Figure 1

6. Insert the needle through the center hole from the *outside* of the book. Pull it through, leaving a 3- or 4-inch-long (8 or 10 cm) tail on the *outside*. Now, from the *inside*, poke the needle through one of the other holes and pull the thread tightly through, being careful to leave the tail hanging out.

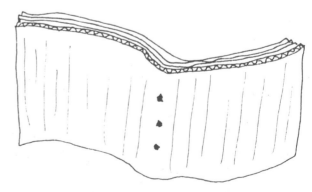

Figure 2

7. Next, from the *outside*, and while holding onto the tail, poke the needle back into the center hole. Pull the thread through to the inside of the book, still holding onto the tail. See Figure 3.

8. Now insert the needle into the remaining hole from the *inside*. Pull the thread tightly and tie it on the *outside* to the tail. Make the tie as close as possible to the center hole. Tie a double bow and trim the ends of the thread. This kind of binding is called *pamphlet binding*.

9. To make the polaire, roll up the book and slip it into the sock. With the book inside the sock, trim off the top of the sock so that only about 3 inches (8 cm) remain above the top of the book.

10. Take the book out of the sock. Use scissors to cut small holes 2 inches (5 cm) down from the top edge of the sock and about 1 inch (2.5 cm) apart all around the sock. See Figure 4.

11. Lace the piece of rope in and out through the holes. See Figure 5. Then tie the two ends of the rope together. Slip the book and a small pen or pencil into the sock, tighten the rope so that the polaire closes, and tie the other end of the rope to your belt or slip it over your shoulder.

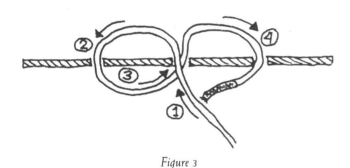

Figure 3

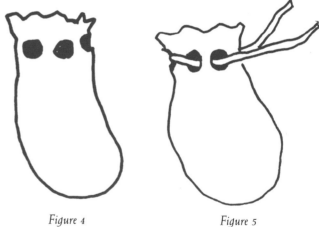

Figure 4   Figure 5

Books that Travel with Their Owners

Throughout history there have been books designed to go places with the people who owned them. These books were small enough to slip into a pocket or small carrying bag. But some books, such as the monk's polaire shown on the right, were a combination book and bag. Monks in the Middle Ages stopped their work to pray many times throughout the day. The polaire saved many a monk a long trip back to his room from the far end of a lavender field when the bell rang for prayer. This little book had an extension of the leather cover that formed a kind of handle from which the book could be hung from the monk's belt. Since monks' belts were also called girdles, this book is sometimes called a girdle book!

Another traveling book was the tiny, beautifully embroidered Elizabethan lady's book. During the 1600s, when Queen Elizabeth I ruled England, ladies of the court carried these little books in fancy pouches or bags. Some of the books contained prayers and some contained collections of uplifting sayings. When a lady of the court had a few minutes during the day to raise her thoughts, she read her little book, which was always with her.

Doctors in the Middle Ages carried books to help them figure out what was wrong with their sick patients. The folding book shown on the left contained information about symptoms and what they might mean, as well as charts that let the doctor try to predict the patient's future. A lot of information could fit into this small book, and when the book was folded into a thin strip, it could easily fit into the doctor's pocket or bag.

Fireworks Show

Celebrate a holiday or a special event in your life by making a pop-up book that explodes with fun and excitement on every page!

WHAT YOU NEED

- Unlined paper, such as typing or copier paper, 8½ by 11 inches (22 by 28 cm)
- Scissors
- Pencil
- Colored pencils or crayons
- Glue stick
- 1 sheet of colored construction paper, 9 by 12 inches (23 by 35 cm)
- Ruler
- Paper clip

WHAT YOU DO

1. Decide which ideas about the celebration you want to show. You might want to show fireworks or special colors, or you might want to show pictures of special stories connected with the holiday. You might want to show some of the foods you enjoy at this time of year, or some special people who help make the holiday what it is. Make a simple drawing of your ideas, and decide which kinds of pop-ups would work best to show them. The different kinds of pop-ups are described in step 2.

2. Fold a sheet of white paper in half from top to bottom and cut it along the fold line. You will now have two pieces of paper, each 5½ inches by 8½ inches (14 by 22 cm). Fold each of these in half, as in Figure 1. This is the first step in making any of the four pop-ups that follow.

To make a pop-up from the center of the page:
a. Draw a straight line from the folded edge halfway across the page. Make this line where you want the bottom of your pop-up to be. See Figure 2.

b. Draw the top edge of the pop-up in whatever shape it needs to be to show the picture you're making. DON'T GO PAST THE MIDDLE OF THE PAGE. Remember that you're drawing half of the object; so, for example, you would draw a flower as shown in Figure 3.

c. Cut along both lines.

d. Open the page and gently pull the pop-up toward you. See Figure 4.

e. Close the page with the pop-up folded on the inside, and press to crease all the folds.

To make two pop-ups from the center of the page:
a. Fold the top and bottom corners of the folded side of the paper down so that they meet, forming two triangles. See Figure 5.

b. Unfold the triangles and draw the top edge of the pop-ups from the folded edges of the paper to the fold lines you have just made. See Figure 6.

c. Cut along the lines you have drawn.

d. Open the page and gently pull the pop-ups toward you along the fold lines you made in step a. See Figure 7.

e. Close the page with the pop-ups folded to the inside. Press hard to make sharp creases.

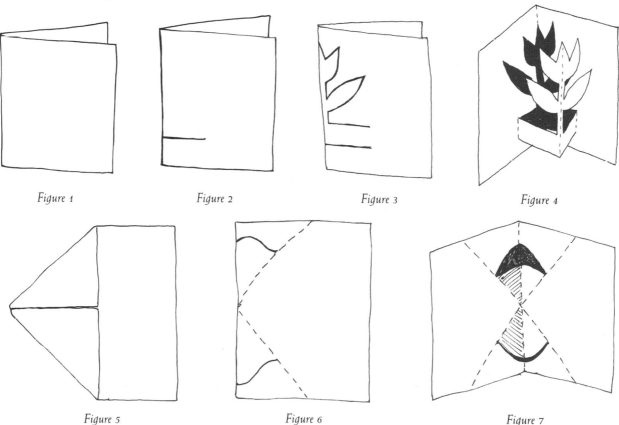

Figure 1   Figure 2   Figure 3   Figure 4

Figure 5   Figure 6   Figure 7

SPECIAL EFFECTS

Imagine a book with rubies and sapphires on the cover and real gold on the edges of the pages. From about the sixth to the 13th century, handwritten and illustrated books with gold or silver covers, encrusted with semi-precious stones, were made for use in church services. In sixth-century Byzantium, books were made with colored leather covers, decorated with jewels and gold, and sometimes with carved ivory portraits of the emperor. Some of these books were so valuable that they were kept in inner rooms of churches, chained to shelves in cabinets.

After the invention of printing, books were no longer considered such rare and precious objects, but bookbinders still had fun with special effects. Besides decorating the covers and spines of books, some bookbinders decorated the edges of the pages. These edges, called *fore-edges*, were painted, marbled, and occasionally carved.

One way of decorating a fore-edge was to close the book and paint or make a shallow carving on the edges of the pages so that the design showed best when the book was closed. Another way, popular with English book designers, was to open the book and paint on the fanned-out edges of the pages. After the watercolor

scene was painted on the fanned-out edges, the book would be closed, then gilded or painted on the closed fore-edge, so that the scene showed only when the book was open. Some artists even painted two scenes on a fore-edge—one that showed when the pages were fanned from left to right, and a second that showed when the pages were fanned from right to left!

The oldest books with fore-edge painting date from around 1650. Many of the techniques used then are still done today, mostly to old books, in the hopes of making them worth a great deal of money on the antiquarian book market.

BOOKS THAT SAVE WORDS, PICTURES, AND IDEAS

~~

Some ideas, words, and pictures are too good to lose. A book is the perfect place to save them. The really clever idea you have today could turn out to be an award-winning invention next year. . . if only you can remember it! When you keep treasured ideas or drawings in a safe place, you'll be able to return to them in a few months or years when you need them. One of the projects in this section is a sketchbook, designed especially for saving pictures. Another is a history book, but not like any one you've ever seen before!

Treasure Chest

Telling the story of your family, your school, your neighborhood, or any other group that you belong to can be an exciting project. Gathering the information is a little like detective work: you will be drawn down surprising pathways and into memorable conversations. Whenever you dig into history, be prepared for mysteries and unsuspected secrets!

The book form in which you record your history can help you tell the story. The form described in this project is based on the idea of hypertext. As you may already know, computers use hypertext. When you read something that uses hypertext, certain words are highlighted in a different color. When you click on those words, the computer gives you more information about that topic. For example, you may be reading about a city you hope to visit. You see some words printed in blue, one of which is "restaurants," and that's something you're curious about. You click on "restaurants" and the screen changes to a listing of all the restaurants near the train station in that city. When you finish reading about the restaurants, you can go back to the main story and continue reading.

Hypertext in your history book will be in the form of little booklets within the main book. Similar to computer hypertext, you will choose some topics to explore in depth. These topics will be set off from the rest of the story so that they need to be read only if the reader wants more details.

WHAT YOU NEED

- ✏ 6 to 8 pieces of copier paper, 8-1/2 inches by 11 inches (22 by 28 cm)
- ✏ Scissors
- ✏ Good-quality paper glue
- ✏ Glue brush
- ✏ Pencil
- ✏ Ruler
- ✏ 2 pieces of cover cardboard, each 5 inches by 6 inches (13 by 15 cm)
- ✏ 2 pieces of decorated cover paper, each 8 inches by 10 inches (20 by 25 cm)
- ✏ Paper clips
- ✏ Awl
- ✏ Sewing needle
- ✏ Waxed cotton thread

WHAT YOU DO

1. Fold each of the sheets of copier paper in half the long way and cut each in half. You will end up with sheets of paper 4¼ inches by 11 inches (11 by 28 cm). Glue these sheets short end to short end in order to get one long sheet of paper that measures 4¼ inches (11 cm) high by however long you want your book to be.

2. After the glue is completely dry, fold the long sheet of paper accordion style. Make each fold the size you want the pages of your book to be. Line up the paper carefully as you fold and press all creases with your fingers. See Figure 1.

3. To make the cover, fold up the accordion. Place it on top of one of the pieces of cover cardboard. Lightly trace around the folded accordion with a pencil. Use the ruler to straighten up your lines. Draw the ruler lines slightly outside the original tracing so that the book cover will be a little bigger than the folded up accordion. Repeat this step to make the back cover.

4. Lay the front cover board on one of the pieces of decorated paper and trace around the outside of it with the pencil. Then add four glue tabs as shown in Figure 2. Repeat this step for the back cover.

5. Put glue all over the inside of one of the sheets of decorated paper. Quickly but carefully lay the cardboard within the outline you drew. Fold the glue tabs over and smooth all of the paper so that it sticks to the cover board with no bubbles. Then glue the other piece of cover paper to the other cover board.

6. Fold the accordion and slip a piece of scrap paper inside the first fold. Put glue all over the outside of the first sheet of the accordion. See Figure 3.

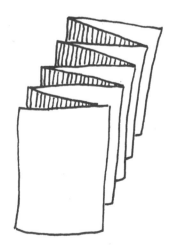

Figure 1

Figure 2

Figure 3

7. Lay the gluey sheet over the inside of the front cover, being careful to center the sheet. See Figure 4.

8. Repeat steps 6 and 7 for the back cover.

9. Make hypertext booklets like this: Cut small sheets of paper, no larger than 2 inches by 4 inches (5 by 10 cm). Fold each stack of sheets in half to make little booklets.

10. Place the hypertext booklets in folds of the accordion wherever you need them to add more details about a person, place, or event. To attach a booklet, use paper clips to hold it in place while you poke three holes in the fold of the booklet and, at the same time, in the accordion fold. See Figure 5.

11. Thread the needle. From the back, insert the needle into the center hole of the booklet. Pull the thread taut, but leave a tail about 4 inches (10 cm) long, which you can hook under one of the paper clips.

12. Insert the needle into the bottom hole and pull the thread taut. From the *outside*, skip over the middle hole and poke the needle into the top hole, making a long stitch.

13. Now, from the *inside*, poke the needle back into the center hole, being sure to come out on the opposite side of the long stitch from the tail. See Figure 6. Tie the thread ends together over the long stitch and trim the thread to ½ inch (1.5 cm).

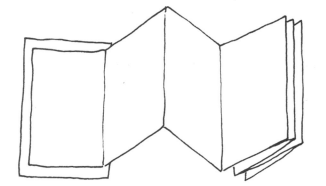

Figure 4

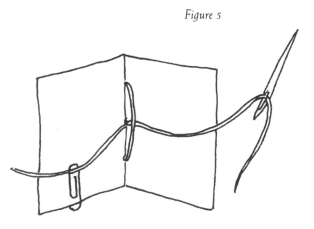

Figure 5

JOHN H. HINCKS

AMILEARD FORTIER

CORRINNE

ARMANTINE FORTIER

JOSEPH A. HINCKS

- LIVED IN NEW ORLEANS

- WEDDING ON OCT 3, 1912

LUCILLE VICTORY DITTMA

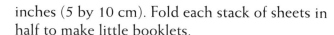

Figure 6

Travel Journal with Secrets

If you're going on a trip, keeping a travel journal can help you remember and enjoy your travels long after they're over. A travel journal can be both a notebook and a sketchbook in which you record in words and pictures the events, places, and surprises you encounter. A travel journal can also be a place to save small souvenirs, such as ticket stubs, photographs, pressed leaves and flowers, brochures, or small maps. This travel journal unfolds like the journey of discovery that traveling can be. Called a tetratetraflexagon, it's easier to make than it is to say! You'll have fun rediscovering the treasures and memories of your travels every time you unfold your book.

WHAT YOU NEED

- 1 piece of paper, 8½ inches by 24 inches (22 by 60 cm); glue two pieces of 8½-inch by 14-inch (22 by 35 cm) copier paper end to end and trim this long sheet to 24 inches (22 cm).
- Ruler
- Pencil
- Scissors
- Cellophane tape
- Materials for writing, drawing, and gluing

WHAT YOU DO

1. Fold the paper in half so that it measures 8½ inches by 12 inches (22 by 30 cm).

2. Fold it in half again so that it measures 8½ inches by 6 inches (22 by 15 cm).

3. Unfold the second fold so that the paper is folded as it was at the end of step 1, but now has creases where you folded it in step 2. See Figure 1.

4. Make marks on the folded edge 2½ inches (6 cm) from the bottom and 2½ inches (6 cm) from the top. Make two other marks on the crease. One should be 2½ inches (6 cm) from the

top, and the other should be 2½ inches (6 cm) from the bottom. See Figure 2.

5. Use the ruler and pencil to connect the dots you have made. See Figure 3.

6. Now carefully cut along the lines that you have drawn. Cut through both thicknesses of paper at one time.

7. Unfold the paper; it should look like Figure 4.

8. Carefully cut from point A on Figure 4 to point B. *Do not cut the other side.*

9. Fold the center strip of paper back so that it folds over the uncut page next to it. See Figure 5.

10. Fold the pages that are marked page 1, 2, and 3 on Figure 5 in and over each other. See Figure 6.

11. Turn the book over. Tape the loose end of the paper strip to the edge of the page nearest it. See Figure 7.

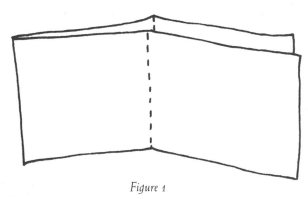

Figure 1

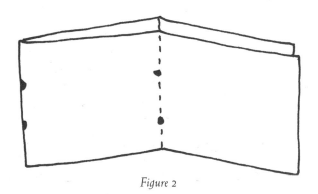

Figure 2

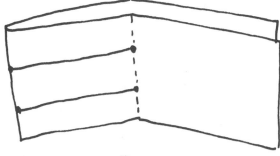

Figure 3

12. To open and close the flexagon, follow these steps:

a. Turn the book over so that the tape is in the back. You are now looking at pages 1 and 2.

b. Push pages 1 and 2 back toward each other. As the pages go back, the center may begin to separate. See Figure 8.

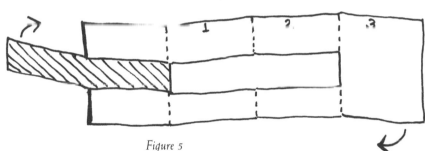

Figure 4

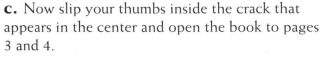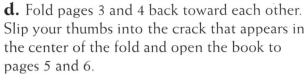

Figure 5

c. Now slip your thumbs inside the crack that appears in the center and open the book to pages 3 and 4.

d. Fold pages 3 and 4 back toward each other. Slip your thumbs into the crack that appears in the center of the fold and open the book to pages 5 and 6.

e. To get back to pages 1 and 2, close pages 5 and 6. At the same time, reach back with your fingers and pull the separating pages at the back forward and closed.

f. Again reach back and pull the separating pages at the back forward. You will now see pages 1 and 2 again. Close them and you will see the cover of the book.

13. Practice opening and closing the book a few times. Write, draw, and glue souvenirs on the pages as you travel. When you get home, your tetratetraflexagon travel journal will help you take your trip again and again in your imagination!

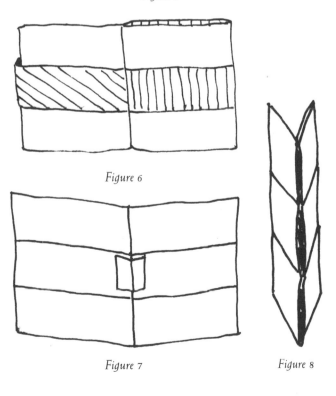

Figure 6

Figure 7   *Figure 8*

Famous Travel Journals

In the days of exploration, long before video cameras and photography, the only way to make a record of what a new place looked like was to draw or paint a picture of it. In the 1500s, when European kings and queens gave money and ships to explorers, they also gave them orders to bring back pictures—and that meant that an artist was needed in the crew.

We still have some of these early travel journals. One of the most carefully drawn and beautifully detailed is that of the Englishman John White. He drew pictures of the Native Americans his group met on the east coast of North America. He also drew and painted plants and animals because so many of these wonders were new to Europeans that words alone could not describe them. His journals are alive with drawings of Native American people and villages, tomatoes and corn plants, and many animals, such as tortoises, gray foxes, squirrels, and Carolina parrots. White's journal is a treasure of information, exotic and wonderful to look at.

Other travelers have kept journals of sights they saw that were new to them, even if they weren't new to anyone else. Americans traveling in Europe during the 19th century captured their memories in the many sketchbook journals they carried. Certain famous sights appeared in many journals long before anyone was able to photograph them: the Spanish steps in Rome, the great cathedrals in France, and the thatched roofed cottages of the English countryside.

Even today a travel journal can preserve memories in a way no photograph can match. In order to draw you have to slow down and really study the subject you're drawing. When you do that, you remember your subject, and your drawing becomes a touchstone that releases the memory for you later.

Secret Garden

A garden notebook helps you keep track of what goes on in your garden each season. This is the place to draw garden plans; write notes about which plants did best in which location; draw your plants as they first sprout and then later as they bud, flower, and form fruit; and even save seeds that you gather from this year's plants to start next year's garden. You can press flowers from your garden, draw the insects that come to visit, write down things you learn about gardening, or save newspaper clippings about gardening. What's more, your secret garden notebook is a way of remembering your garden even on the coldest days of winter. And when spring comes again, your notebook can help you start your new garden, too!

61

WHAT YOU NEED

- ↪ 2 pieces of cardboard or chipboard, each 6 inches by 9 inches (15 by 23 cm)
- ↪ Wallpaper, self-adhesive shelf paper, or colored pages from seed catalogs
- ↪ Scissors
- ↪ Good-quality paper glue
- ↪ Glue brush
- ↪ Craft knife
- ↪ 10 sheets of copier paper (you can add more as you need it)
- ↪ 5 sheets of grid paper
- ↪ Hole puncher
- ↪ Awl
- ↪ Pen or pencil
- ↪ Several plastic sandwich bags with self-sealing closures
- ↪ 2 notebook rings, 1- or 1½-inch (2.5 or 4 cm) in diameter
- ↪ 1 piece of string or yarn about 2 feet (60 cm) long

WHAT YOU DO

1. You will need to make two book covers. Place one piece of cardboard on the wrong side of a piece of wallpaper (or whatever you are using for cover paper). Trim the paper so it's about 1½ inches (4 cm) bigger than the cardboard on all sides. Center the cardboard on the paper and draw a pencil line all around it.

2. Brush glue onto the cover paper inside the pencil outline of the cover. Be sure to completely coat this area with glue. Lay the piece of cardboard down on the glue, making sure that it's inside the pencil line on all four sides. See Figure 1.

3. Use scissors or the craft knife to trim each corner. See Figure 2.

4. Place the cover on your work surface so that the decorative paper side is down and you can see the cardboard. Put glue on each of the four flaps, and then fold each flap up to glue it to the cover. Smooth or burnish both sides of the cover to be sure the paper is sticking well to all surfaces. See Figure 3.

5. Cut a piece of cover paper to fit ¼ inch (1 cm) inside the edges of the cover; this will be your *endpaper*. Glue it to the inside of the cover so that you can no longer see the cardboard. See Figure 4.

6. Repeat steps 1 through 5 for the other cover.

7. Cut the pieces of copier paper and the grid paper in half crosswise so each piece measures 5½ inches by 8 inches (14 by 20 cm). Stack the sheets.

8. Punch two holes in the front cover about 1 inch (2.5 cm) in from each short side and ½ inch (1.5 cm) in from the long edge. You may need to start the holes with the awl and widen them with the craft knife if the paper-covered cardboard is too thick for the hole puncher.

9. Pick up the first five sheets from the stack of paper and carefully place this short stack under the front cover so that the paper is butted up against the long side edge of the cover. The holes on the cover should be to the left. Use a pencil to

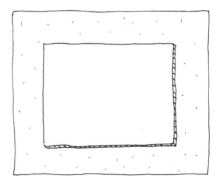

Figure 1

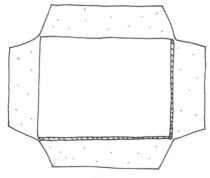

Figure 2

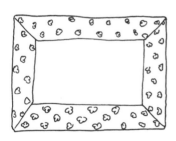

Figure 3

11. Stack up the front cover and all of the paper, arranged so that all the holes are lined up. Place this stack on top of the other cover. Use a pencil to mark the centers of the holes. Remove the front cover and all of the paper, and punch two holes on the back cover where you have made pencil marks.

12. Place one plastic bag at a time over the front cover, lining up the bottom of the bag with the edge that has holes punched in it. Use the awl to punch holes in the plastic bags to line up with the holes in the cover.

You can slide pressed flowers into the bags and then seal them up, or wrap small seeds in sheets of waxed paper and slide the waxed paper envelopes into the plastic bags when you want to save seeds. Put a label made of tape on the outside of the plastic bag to identify and date the seeds or pressed flowers.

13. Arrange the two covers, the plastic bags, and the pages so that all holes line up. Slip a notebook ring into each hole, and lock each ring closed.

14. Tie one end of the piece of string or yarn to one of the rings. Tie the other end to a pen or pencil so that it will be handy when you need to record something.

mark where the holes should be punched on the paper. See Figure 5.

10. Carefully remove the cover, and use the hole puncher to punch holes through all five sheets at one time. Repeat steps 9 and 10 until all of the paper has been punched.

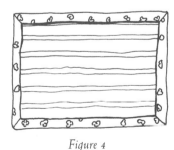

Figure 4

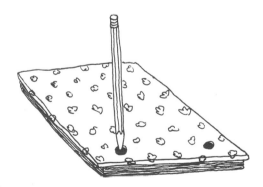

Figure 5

Medieval Herbals

An *herbal* is a book that features names, descriptions, and usually illustrations of plants. In the Middle Ages, herbals were important medical books. In the 12th century, if you had a bad cold your mother probably went into the woods to pick certain plants, and came home to brew them in a pot for you. She might also have made a poultice of leaves to put on your chest. If you were very sick, the village herb wife, or a monk from the local monastery who grew herbs, might have been called because they had better knowledge of which plants would make you well.

Some of the early herbals that we know of come from China. One, Shen Nong's *Classic of Materia Medica*, dating from the first or second century, lists 365 healing herbs. Much older than that is a fragment of papyrus from Egypt dating back to 1700 B.C. that describes some of the same

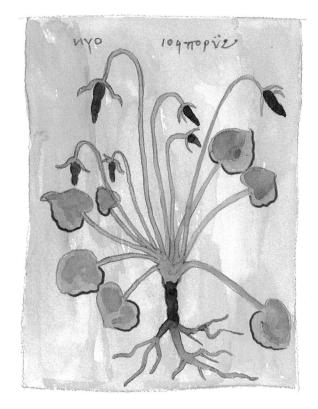

herbs that we use today to cure illnesses.

In the Middle Ages herbals were written in part to help ordinary people identify the plants that would help them heal wounds or illnesses. The idea was that people could find their own herbs in the woods or in hedgerows, and not have to pay for expensive and sometimes dangerous medicines sold by specially trained people, called apothecaries. Herbals were usually very carefully illustrated because sometimes a useful plant looked very similar to a poisonous one. People gathering their own herbs needed accurate information. This was one type of book in which accuracy was truly a matter of life or death.

Picture Gallery

Artists sometimes make their own sketchbooks. They know that the only way they can find a sketchbook with the kind and size of paper they like is to make their own. The sketchbook that you will make in this project has a secret compartment hidden in the cover—a perfect place to tuck a pencil and any small treasures you pick up while you're out sketching.

WHAT YOU NEED
- ⇢ 1 sheet of your favorite drawing paper, at least 17 inches by 22 inches (43 by 55 cm)
- ⇢ Scrap of cardboard
- ⇢ Awl
- ⇢ 1 piece of waxed cotton thread, 3 feet (.9 m) long
- ⇢ Large-eyed sewing needle
- ⇢ Scissors
- ⇢ 1 piece of heavy cover paper, about 17 inches by 22 inches (43 by 55 cm)
- ⇢ 1 piece of lighter weight (but strong) paper, 8½ inches by 11 inches (22 by 28 cm)
- ⇢ Pencil
- ⇢ Ruler
- ⇢ Good-quality paper glue
- ⇢ Glue brush

WHAT YOU DO

1. Fold the large sheet of paper like an accordion three times with the folds going down the long direction of the page. See Figure 1.

2. Fold the long folded sheet of paper again, this time from side to side. See Figure 2.

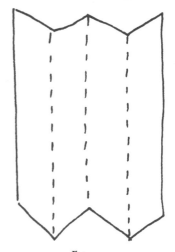

Figure 1

3. Fold the folded piece of paper one more time from side to side. See Figure 3.

4. Press all of the folds hard. Open only the last fold that you made. This fold will become the inside fold of the finished book. Protect your work surface with the scrap of cardboard. Use the awl to poke three holes in the fold, poking through all the pages at once. See Figure 4.

5. Thread the needle, but don't make a knot in it. From the *outside*, insert the needle into the center hole. Pull the thread until a tail about 5 inches (13 cm) long is left hanging out. Hold onto the tail as you continue sewing so that it doesn't pull through.

6. Poke the needle from the *inside* into either one of the other holes and pull the thread gently tight. Hold onto the tail!

7. Now insert the needle from the *outside* into the last hole, skipping over the center hole to make a long stitch. See Figure 5.

8. From the *inside*, poke the needle back into the center hole, being careful to come out of the hole on the opposite side of the long stitch from the tail. See Figure 6.

9. Cut the thread so that it's as long as the tail, and tie the two ends together into a small knot over the long stitch. Clip the thread ends to about 1 inch (2.5 cm).

10. Use scissors to trim the folds from the three unstitched sides. If your paper is rather heavy, try opening the booklet before trimming it. Be sure to cut off all of the folds from these sides. Check

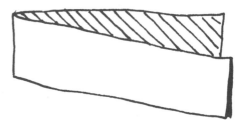

Figure 2

Figure 3

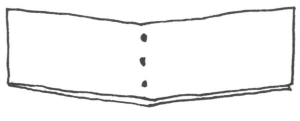

Figure 4

by turning all the pages. The little booklet you have just made is called a signature.

11. To make the cover, place the sewn edge of the signature centered against one of the shorter edges of the cover page. Lightly draw around the signature with a pencil. See Figure 7.

12. Now move the signature and put the sewn edge against the shortest pencil line you just drew, as shown in Figure 8. Use the ruler to redraw these lines nice and straight and to add 4 inches (10 cm) onto the short end of the shape you just drew. See Figure 8. Cut out the cover only along the outside lines you drew in Figure 8.

13. Line up the signature and one short edge of the cover. Fold the cover around the signature. You will have one cover that fits and the other sticking out around 4 inches (10 cm). You will use the extra part of the cover to make a flap to keep the secret compartment closed. You can either round the edges of this flap, cut them into a point, or leave them alone. See Figure 9.

14. Open up the book to the inside of the front cover (the short cover is the front cover). Slip the piece of 8½-inch by 11-inch (22 by 28 cm) paper under the back cover to measure for the secret compartment. The fold of the book should be lined up with the long edge of the paper. Draw lightly in pencil around the three edges of the book as shown in Figure 10.

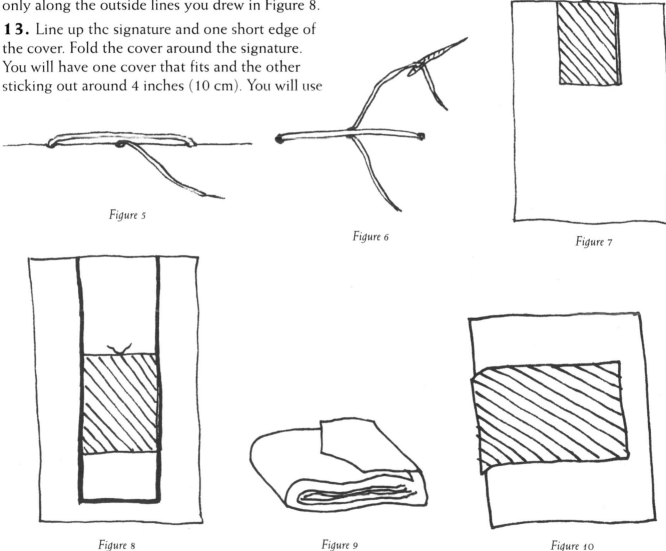

Figure 5

Figure 6

Figure 7

Figure 8

Figure 9

Figure 10

15. Make a straight line all the way across the end of the book and trim the paper that sticks out past the end of the book. See Figure 11.

16. Make three accordion folds about ½ inch (1.5 cm) apart on each of the sides that overlap the sides of the signature. The folds should divide the space into three equal long, skinny spaces. See Figure 12.

17. Carefully glue the *outside* of the front page of the signature to the *inside* of the front cover. Then glue the *outside* of the back page of the signature to the *back* of the secret compartment. Place the bottom of the secret compartment against the fold in the cover so that the entire last page covers the entire back of the secret compartment. See Figure 13.

18. Put glue on the outermost folds of the secret compartment and press these against the edges of the back cover. Press the folds closed so that they are glued to the entire edges of the back cover, beginning at the fold. Several inches of the cover should stick out beyond the secret compartment. This flap wraps around to the front to help keep the secret compartment closed. See Figure 14.

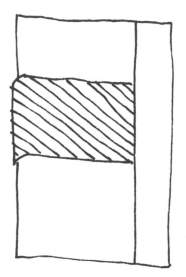

Figure 11

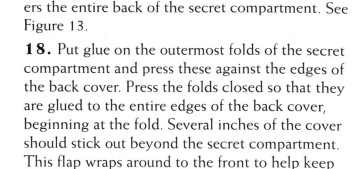

Figure 12

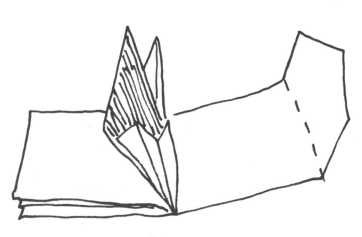

Figure 13

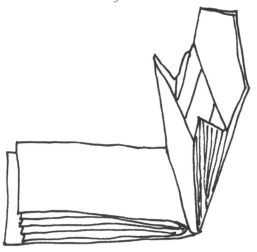

Figure 14

THE CASE OF THE MIXED UP SKETCHBOOKS

Like many other artists, the famous 19th-century Dutch artist Vincent Van Gogh often carried and drew in a sketchbook to remember things he saw, study certain subjects, try out compositions, and, in general, think on paper. After Van Gogh died, his drawings and paintings were sought after, and some of his sketchbooks were cut apart so that individual pages could be sold as drawings.

In recent years people studying Van Gogh's life and work realized that if his sketchbooks could be put back together we could learn many things, such as how many sketches there were in the first place, even if all of them couldn't be found. A reassembled sketchbook could also tell something about the order in which Van Gogh made the drawings, and that would help people date them. It could even tell which of his many drawings were sketches and which were made as finished drawings

But how to reconstruct the sketchbooks? Call in the art detectives! One of the detectives on this case was a man named Johannes Van der Wolk. Using sleuthlike deductions from clues that would have baffled even Sherlock Holmes, Van der Wolk managed to reconstruct four of Van Gogh's sketchbooks and parts of three others.

How did he do it? Here are some of the clues he worked with: the size of the pages that remained from the seven known sketchbooks; the kind of paper in each sketchbook; the position of the staples or stitches that originally held the books together; and marks on the pages, such as stains and pencil marks.

To decide the order of the pages, Van der Wolk made models of the sketchbooks. These let him see which pages would touch each other in the center. Sometimes he was able to match a mark or glue trace on one page with one on another page. He matched stains on pages, kinds of pencil or ink used from page to page, and parts of drawings that began on one page and continued on the next. In some sketches the edges of the pages had been painted or trimmed square, or even trimmed in a round corner. Van der Wolk was able to match these painted or cut edges. What a remarkable piece of detective work!

To learn more about Johannes Van der Wolk's project, read his book, *The Seven Sketchbooks of Vincent Van Gogh*, published by Harry N. Abrams, Inc. and Thames and Hudson, Ltd. in 1987.

The Schraubthaler or Coin Book

One of the strangest books ever made is one that no one even knew was a book for several hundred years after it was created. During the 1960s, a coin collector in England had an old commemorative coin dated 1639. It was about as large as an American silver dollar and was known as a *thaler*. On one side of the coin was a portrait of a Swedish king and on the other side was a view of the city of Augsburg, Germany. This was nothing special as far as old coins go. But one day the coin collector noticed something strange about the coin: a thin, hairline crack ran all around the outer rim. The coin collector carefully used a tiny flat screwdriver to widen the crack, and suddenly, to his great surprise, the two halves of the coin came apart and a tiny round book fell out!

The little book has 17 round pages joined to each other by flat ribbons. Each "page" of the book is a tiny painting, or miniature, of a scene from the life of Martin Luther, a German monk who lived from 1483 until 1546 and founded the Protestant church. The coin is now known as the Schraubthaler, or screw thaler, because it is a coin that opens by unscrewing the two halves.

Books That Help Us Think and Make Sense of Experiences

 iscussing a problem with a friend is a good way to think about it or solve it. Another approach is to write about the problem or situation in the form of a story. The act of writing often helps us to know what we know and understand what we feel. Making a book in which you express the situation in words and pictures can help you sort things out. One of the projects in this section is a way to have a healthy argument or debate with a friend. Another helps you play with many possibilities and arrangements of ideas.

Dos à Dos

Dos à dos is a French expression meaning a couch or a carriage that holds two people sitting back to back. When two people sit back to back, they see different things or they see the same thing from two different points of view. Imagine that you and your friend are sitting back to back on a park bench. Your friend, who is facing the swings, says, "This park is full of little kids playing on the swings!" You, who are facing the fountain, say, "No, it's not! It's full of old people sitting on benches around the fountain and dozing in the sun!" Who's right? You both are, because you are looking at different parts of the park.

Now imagine that the mayor of your town wants to build a new, larger bridge across the river. One group of people thinks this is a terrible idea; a new bridge will cost a lot of money, and the old bridge seems fine. The other group thinks the old bridge isn't wide enough for all the traffic that crosses the river every day, and a new bridge is essential. Who's right? Both groups may be; each is looking at the question from a different point of view. So how can anyone decide what to do? The best thing would be to get as much information as possible from all points of view and then make a decision.

A dos à dos is also a kind of book that can express two points of view. Since the book is really two books in one (or three books or more—you decide), there is room for each person's point of view or story. Make a dos à dos whenever you and your friend have different points of view that you want to tell about, or when you can think of two or more ways to do something, or when several people have different stories about the same idea, or even when you want to think through something carefully before making a decision.

WHAT YOU NEED

- Paper for each section of the book; each sheet should be wide enough to be folded in half, making two sheets in one.
- Cover paper; for a two-point-of-view dos à dos, this paper should be the same height as the text pages, and as wide as 3 text pages; for a three-point-of-view book it needs to be as wide as 4 text pages, and so on.
- Several large paper clips
- Ruler
- 1 piece of corrugated cardboard (to protect your work table)
- Awl
- Waxed thread, 4 feet (1.2 m) long
- Sewing needle
- Scissors
- Materials for writing text and illustrating the book
- Beads to decorate the binding (optional)

WHAT YOU DO

1. Fold all the text pages in half sideways. Crease them firmly; then slide them inside each other to make two booklets, or signatures. If you are making a three- or four-part dos à dos, divide the pages into three or four signatures.

2. Lay a signature on top of the cover sheet at the left end. Mark by scoring with a paper clip along the right edge of the signature. See Figure 1.

3. Move the signature over so that it's lined up along the first line that you scored, and score another line at the right edge of the signature. See Figure 2. Repeat this step. If your book will have more than two signatures, repeat this step until you have scored a line for each signature

Figure 1

Figure 2

that will be in the book. Check to be sure each section of the cover is the same size.

4. Fold the cover on the first scored line. Now turn the cover sheet over and fold it on the next scored line. When you look at the cover sheet from the edge, it should look like a letter Z.

Figure 3

See Figure 3. If you have more than two scores, continue folding back and forth until you have several Zs.

5. Slip a signature into the first fold. Open out the book and place it on a piece of corrugated cardboard to protect the work table. Paper clip the signature to the cover so that the crease of the signature is nested inside the crease of the cover. Use an awl to poke a hole right in the center of the crease. Then poke another hole midway between the top of the crease and the first hole. Poke a third hole midway between the bottom of the crease and the middle hole. See Figure 4.

6. Unclip the first signature from the cover and turn the cover over. Clip the second signature to the back side of the cover so that the crease of the second signature nests inside of the second crease of the cover. Poke three holes in this crease as you did in step 5. See Figure 5.

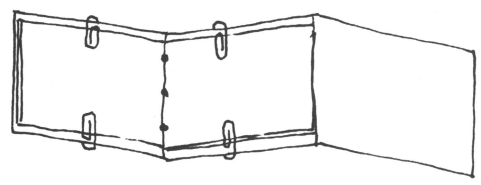

Figure 4

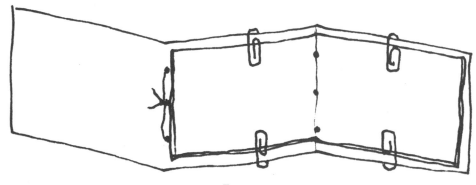

Figure 5

hole, and poke the needle into the bottom hole. Pull the thread firmly. Poke the needle back into the middle hole. You will notice that the tail of the thread is on one side of the crease. Be sure to come out of the middle hole on the opposite side of the thread from the tail. See Figure 6.

8. Tie the tail to the end of the thread across the long stitch. Clip the ends of the thread. See Figure 7. If you want, slip a bead onto one end of the thread before you tie it.

9. Repeat steps 7 and 8 for all other signatures.

10. Fold the book back and forth so that you can open one signature from the front and one from the back (if you have made a three- or four-part book, you can open all signatures by turning the book back and forth).

11. Write the text and make the illustrations.

12. Decorate the covers.

Here are a few wild ideas to consider. As with any book, you can change the shape, size, and materials of this book. If you need some extra long pages, cut some text pages longer than the others, and make fold outs. Cut some pages taller than the others and make fold-downs. Make fold-ins on the front and back covers. Add some pop-ups.

7. Thread the needle but don't knot the thread. Poke the needle from the outside of the cover through the middle hole of the paper-clipped signature and cover. Pull the thread until a tail about 5 inches (13 cm) long is left. Slip the tail under one of the paper clips to hold it in place. Next poke the needle into the top hole and pull the thread firmly (but leave the tail clipped in place). Come out of the top hole, cross over the middle

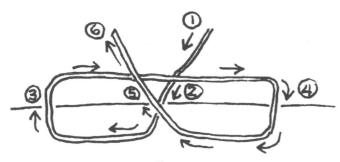

Figure 6

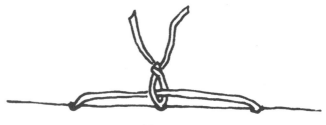

Figure 7

Labyrinth

A labyrinth is a maze, a complex structure of interconnected paths. In a way, a person's life can be said to be a labyrinth, since each person is complicated and follows many paths. This book has three paths that are separate but connected. It's a good format for telling someone's life story or biography because different parts of the person's story can be written or illustrated on the different paths. The book looks as rich and complicated as a long life!

WHAT YOU NEED
- ❧ Several sheets of copier paper, 8½ inches by 11 inches (14 by 22 cm), white or light colored
- ❧ Scissors
- ❧ 2 pieces of cover cardboard, each about 4½ inches by 3 inches (11 by 8 cm)
- ❧ Pencil
- ❧ Ruler
- ❧ Craft knife
- ❧ 2 pieces of decorative cover paper
- ❧ Good-quality paper glue
- ❧ Glue brush
- ❧ Pens, markers, color copies of photographs, and other materials for writing text and illustrating the book

WHAT YOU DO

1. A good first step is to gather all the photographs and information that you have about the person. You could interview the person to find out important information as well as interesting stories. After you have all the materials, spread them out on a table so you can get an idea of how much space you are going to need and also how you could divide up the information and materials. For instance, you could write a time line of the person's life along the top edge of the book. Or you could make a path of photographs through the middle of the book. You could also tell special stories that give a good picture of the person on the bottom edge of the book. If you want, you could use both sides of the book, which would give you six paths.

2. Once you have planned the book, the next step is to decide how many pages you need. Then cut several sheets of copier paper in half the long way, and glue these 4¼-inch by 11-inch (12 by 22 cm) sheets together into one long strip.

3. Fold this long strip back and forth into a accordion that has as many pages as you need. Make all pages (or folds) exactly the same size so that when the accordion is folded, it will measure 4¼ inches (12 cm) by however wide you have made each page. See Figure 1.

4. Now you are ready to make the front and back covers. Place the folded accordion on top of a piece of cover cardboard and trace around it with a pencil. To make the cover slightly larger than the accordion, use a ruler to draw straight lines just outside the traced lines. See Figure 2. Ask an adult to help you cut the cardboard with a craft knife and a ruler. Repeat this step to cut out the back cover.

5. To cover the cover boards, follow steps 1 through 6 on page 62.

6. To divide the accordion into paths, first make a narrow accordion, just as you did in steps 2 and 3 on this page. Make this strip about one-third as

Figure 1

The photographs in the accordion book show handwritten text including:

"MY GRANDMOTHER'S LIFE STORY"

"Lucille Victory Dittmann was born November 11, 1918 — Armistice Day."

"She was born and lived in New Orleans with her parents and six brothers and sisters."

"She went to Catholic school at first, but had to transfer to public schools when the Great Depression hit."

"In 1935, Lucille met Carle Crozier. She didn't like him at first, but..."

"Her parents gave her the middle name "Victory" as a remembrance of the day she was born."

"...her brothers worked as an account executive for Merrill Lynch."

"In high school, Lucille played varsity basketball and won many honors."

"...they went on to get married in 1941."

tall as the main accordion and almost as long. Make the folds of this accordion half as deep as the folds of the main accordion.

7. Fold up the small accordion; then fold up the main accordion. Lay the small accordion on top of the main accordion, centered between top and bottom. See Figure 3.

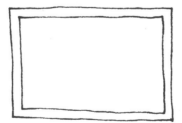

Figure 2

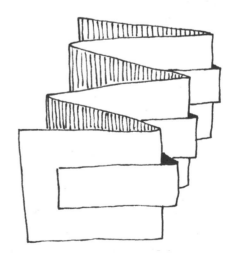

Figure 3

8. Mark the top and bottom of the small accordion. Now you need to cut out the shape shown in Figure 4 from each page of the main accordion. The easiest way to do this is to cut them all at once. Ask an adult to help you draw the shape and cut it out with a craft knife. Be sure that the tall end of the shape is the same height as the small accordion.

9. At this point, you should write the text and glue on or draw the illustrations. Be sure to leave the first and last 3 inches (8 cm) of the small accordion blank.

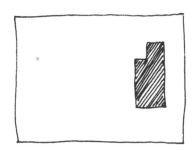

Figure 4

10. To put the book together, begin by gluing the main accordion to the covers. Close the main accordion. Place a piece of scrap paper under the top sheet for protection, and then brush glue all over the top sheet. Lay the gluey sheet centered over the side of a cover that is not completely covered by decorative paper. See Figure 5. Repeat this step for the back cover. Press down to smooth out all bubbles from the pages that you glued to the cover boards.

11. Lace the small accordion through the cutout spaces in the main accordion. Carefully brush glue onto the folded-under end pages of the small accordion, and press them to the inside covers in the correct position. See Figure 6.

12. Fold up the book after all glue has dried, making any adjustments necessary so that the book opens and closes smoothly.

Figure 5

Figure 6

Imaginary World

When you open a book, you walk into an imaginary world. This book is simple to make. It has strong covers and a sturdy binding—a good place to hold stories, poems, or even a novel.

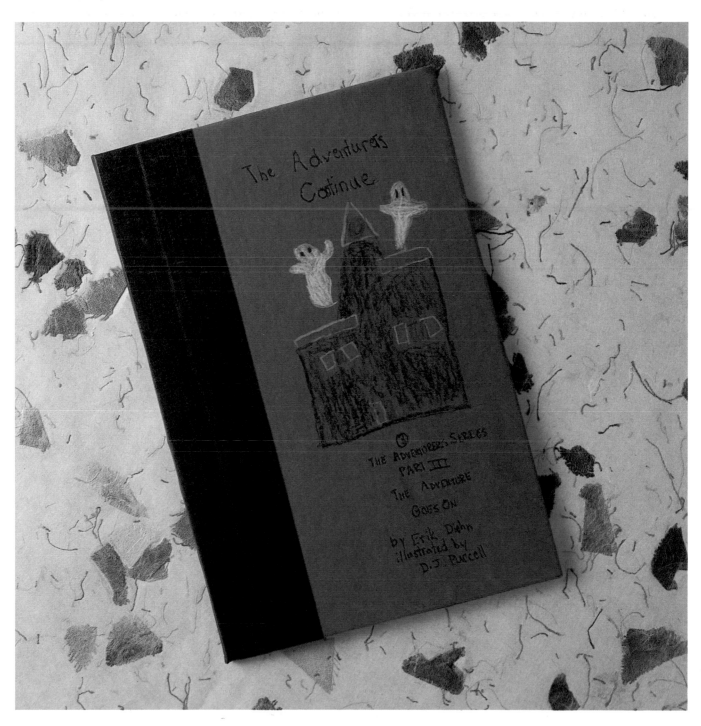

WHAT YOU NEED

- Copier paper, 8½ inches by 11 inches (22 by 28 cm)
- Materials for writing text and illustrating the book
- 1 sheet of heavy colored paper, such as construction paper, 8½ inches by 11 inches (22 by 28 cm) or slightly larger
- Several paper clips
- Awl
- Sewing needle
- 1 piece of waxed cotton thread or dental floss, 3 to 4 feet (.9 to 1.2 m) long
- Scissors
- 2 pieces of heavy cardboard or chipboard, each 6 inches by 9 inches (15 by 23 cm)
- 2 sheets of heavy decorated or colored paper, such as wrapping paper, wallpaper sample, or construction paper
- Good-quality paper glue
- Glue brush
- Duct tape

simplify cover

WHAT YOU DO

1. Decide how many sheets of paper it will take to write and illustrate your story. You will be folding the copier paper in half, so each sheet will be 8½ inches by 5½ inches (22 by 14 cm). It's a very good idea to make a practice book or dummy by folding sheets of scratch paper and mapping out where the illustrations and text will go in the finished book. Once you know where everything will go, fold good paper in half and slip the sheets inside one another to make a signature. Write the text and do the illustrations before going any further.

2. Once the book is written and illustrated, open the signature to the center fold. Fold the sheet of heavy colored paper around the outside of the signature; this soft cover will become the two sheets that you will glue to the covers to bind the book. Paper clip all the pages of the opened signature together so they don't move around. Use the awl to punch five holes, about 1 inch (2.5 cm) apart, in the crease of the signature. See Figure 1.

3. Thread the needle with 3 feet (.9 m) of thread or dental floss. Do not tie a knot.

4. Figure 2 shows how to stitch together the pages and the endpapers. Insert the needle into the center hole from the *outside*. Pull the thread through, and slip a tail about 5 inches (13 cm) long under one of the paper clips. Next poke the needle into the next hole up from the center. Pull the thread to the *outside* and insert the needle into the top hole. Pull the thread to the *inside* and insert the needle back into the second hole down. Again pull the thread through and poke the needle back into the center hole. Next, pull the thread and insert the needle into the next hole down from the center. Pull the thread and poke

the needle into the bottom hole. Pull the thread and then insert the needle into the next hole up. Pull the thread through. The needle will be on the *outside*, the same side as the tail. Tie the tail to the thread as it comes out of its hole so that you have a tight stitch. Clip the tail and thread end to ¼ inch (1 cm).

5. To make the cover, you need to cover the chipboard or cardboard with decorative paper. Place one cover board on a piece of decorative paper and trace around the board with a pencil. Draw glue tabs as in Figure 3. Cut out the cover paper. Repeat this step for the other cover board.

6. Brush glue all over the inside of the first sheet of cover paper. Carefully place the cover board centered between the glue tabs. See Figure 3. Fold the tabs up around the cover. Press and smooth all the paper to get rid of any bubbles. Some wrinkles will flatten as the glue dries. Repeat this step for the other cover. See Figure 4.

7. Lay the two covers on a table with their insides facing up. Cut a piece of duct tape about 12 inches (30 cm) long. Place the tape on the

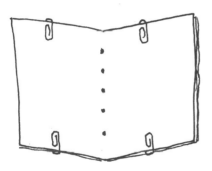

Figure 1

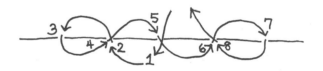

Figure 2

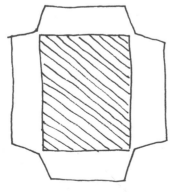

Figure 3

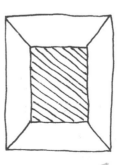

Figure 4

table sticky side up. Carefully place the cover boards on the tape with a space at least ¼ inch (1 cm) wide between them. See Figure 5. Fold the extra duct tape down over the covers. See Figure 6.

8. Put a piece of scrap paper under the colored piece of paper at the front of the signature to protect the first page of the signature. Brush glue all over the top side of the colored piece of paper. Lay the gluey paper over the inside of the front cover and press the paper all over. Be sure to press

it into the creases near the tape between the cover boards. Repeat this step for the back cover. See Figure 7. Open and close the book a few times and continue to flatten any bubbles.

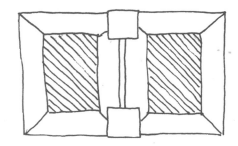

Figure 6

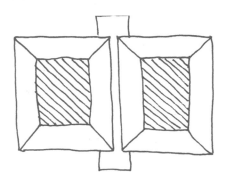

Figure 5

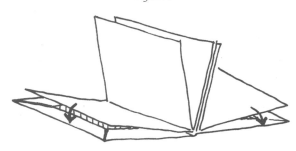

Figure 7

The Biggest, The Smallest—A Collection of Record-Breaking Books

By now you know that a book can come in many different shapes and sizes, but did you know that there are some books that are taller than a very tall human? In 1985, book artist Barbara DeGenevieve made a book with pages that are each 3 by 7 feet (.9 by 2.5 m)! The book's covers are made from hollow-core doors. The pages, made of linen, are held to the covers with nails and three metal hinges. It takes two people to turn the pages of this giant!

At the other extreme, *The Guinness Book of Records* lists a book that measures 1/25 by 1/25 of an inch! The pages are so small that they can be turned only with a needle! The book contains the children's story, *Old King Cole*, and was published in 1985 by The Gleniffer Press in Scotland.

The Guinness Book lists some other record holders:

-The oldest handwritten book found in one piece is a book of psalms discovered at Beni Suef in Egypt. The book is about 1600 years old.

-The oldest mechanically printed book is the Dharani scroll, found in South Korea in 1966. The scroll was printed from carved wooden blocks, and is at least 1200 years old.

-The first large-scale printing on paper took place in Japan in the year 770 when the Empress Shotoku ordered the printing of a million paper prayer scrolls. Each scroll, or *dharani,* was placed in its own three-story wooden pagoda, only 4½ inches (11 cm) high. It took six years to complete the project, not all that long when you consider that all the printing was done by hand from carved wooden blocks. Ten temples in Japan each gave away 100,000 of the pagodas!

-An interesting record (also in *The Guinness Book*) is that the all-time best selling book (other than noncopyrighted books such as the *Bible* and the *Koran*) is *The Guinness Book of Records*, first published in October 1955 by the Guinness Brewery in England. The book has been published in 38 different languages. As of April 1996, more than 79 million copies had been sold!

-And finally, the most overdue library book ever returned in the United States was a book on diseases checked out in 1823 from the University of Cincinnati Medical Library. It was returned December 7, 1968 by the borrower's great-grandson. The fine was $2,264, but the library said "Never mind!"

Exquisite Corpse

Many years ago there was a group of artists and writers who called themselves the Surrealists. The Surrealists were great experimenters and game players, and one of the games they made up and liked to play at their parties was called "The Exquisite Corpse." What a strange name for a game! And what's an exquisite corpse anyway? A beautiful dead body?

Actually, the name of the game tells something about the game itself. It was a game of chance and unpredictable happenings. Here's how they played it: Someone would fold a piece of paper into several long, skinny folds so that only one fold at a time could be seen. The first person would write a word or a sentence on the first fold, then fold the paper so that no one could see what he or she had written. The next person would write another word or sentence on the next fold, fold it over so that the writing was hidden, and pass the paper on to the next person, and so on. When everyone had written on the paper it was unfolded, and the Surrealists read the resulting poem or story. Of course it wouldn't make sense most of the time, but often words would be combined in interesting ways that no one would have thought of had the poem or story been written in the ordinary way. The first time they played this game, the first three words were "the exquisite corpse," and everyone liked the sound of that, so that's what they called the game.

Exquisite Corpse can also be played with drawings. For example, the first person can draw a head, the next person a neck, the next person shoulders, and so on, until all the parts of a body are drawn. When the paper is unfolded, the results are always very interesting and wonderfully funny!

You can make a book that works like a game of Exquisite Corpse. It's fun to make this book with other people so that you can get lots of ideas to put on the pages. Then, when you make different arrangements, you'll have some really exquisite corpses!

WHAT YOU NEED

- 1 piece of poster paper or other heavy paper, 8-1/2 inches by 11 inches (22 by 28 cm)
- 10 sheets of copier paper, 8-1/2 inches by 11 inches (22 by 28 cm)
- Several paper clips
- Awl
- Large-eyed sewing needle
- 1 piece of heavy thread, about 5 feet (1.5 m) long
- Scissors
- 1 piece of corrugated cardboard (to protect your work table)
- Craft knife
- Metal ruler
- Markers, crayons, or other media for illustration

OR

- Pen or pencil for writing text

WHAT YOU DO

1. Fold the cover paper and all the sheets of copier paper in half so that each folded sheet is 5½ inches by 8½ inches (22 by 28 cm).

2. Decide whether you want to make pictures or a story for your exquisite corpse. If you want to make pictures, decide how you want to divide the body: into head and neck, shoulders and chest and arms, hips and legs and feet (three parts), or into head and neck, shoulders and chest and arms, hips, legs, feet (five parts).

If you want to make a story exquisite corpse, decide on parts, for example: describe the setting, introduce a character, make that character do something, introduce another character, make the characters have a problem, solve the problem (six parts); or describe the place or setting, introduce two characters, make something happen, let the characters have a conversation,

begin, put all the folded pages inside each other and then inside the folded cover, and bump the edges against a table to line up all the pages evenly inside the cover. Put a few paper clips along the right-hand open side of the book to hold everything in place.

introduce another character, let all three characters solve the problem, write an ending (seven parts). You can divide your exquisite corpse into as many parts as you want, but stick to no more than eight parts or the pages will be too skinny to write or draw on.

3. After you know how many parts you will need, write down your list of parts and put it away for now.

4. The next step is binding the book. We will use a side-sewn binding called a *Japanese stab binding*. To

5. Use the awl to punch holes along the left, folded edge around ½ inch (1.5 cm) in from the fold and ½ inch (1.5 cm) apart from each other. See Figure 1. Consider how many parts your exquisite corpse will be divided into, and be sure to have at least two holes in each part.

6. Thread the needle and insert it into the top hole. Pull the thread all the way until a tail about 4 inches (10 cm) long is left. Slip the tail under one of the paper clips to hold it. There is no need to knot the thread.

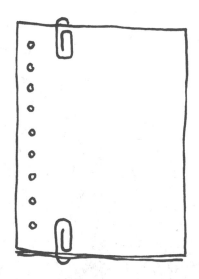

Figure 1

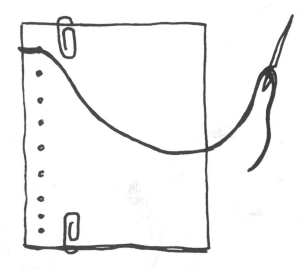

Figure 2

7. Wrap the thread around the outside of the spine and come back into the same hole. See Figure 2. The needle will now be on the back side of the book.

8. Poke the needle, from the back, into the next hole down. The needle will come out on the front of the book. Pull the thread around the outside of the book and then poke the needle back into the same (second) hole. Now the needle is on the front of the book.

9. Poke the needle, from the front, into the next hole down (the third), and repeat step 8. Continue repeating steps 8 and 9 until you have sewed in each hole. The front of your book will look like Figure 3.

10. To fill in the gaps between the stitches, wrap

the thread around the outside of the book, and put the needle back into the last hole. Next, simply put the needle in and out of each hole. As you sew, you will be filling in the spaces on both the front and back of the book. There's no need to wrap the side of the book since you already did that. Tie off the thread to the tail, and clip the ends.

11. Get your list of how many parts you will divide your exquisite corpse into. Ask an adult to help you cut each page into as many pieces as there will be parts. You can cut several pages at one time. To do so, slip a piece of corrugated cardboard under the pages you are cutting to protect the back cover of the book. You should NOT cut the covers. Start the cuts about ¼ inch (1 cm) in from the stitching of your book. When you finish cutting, each page of your book should be divided into several small pages. It's very important that all the pages be exactly the same size, so be careful to make the cuts right on top of one another. The best way to do this is to cut several pages at one time.

12. Now for the really fun part. Think of each part of the corpse as a small book. You will now write or draw as many different kinds of whatever that part is going to be as you have pages in the book. For example, if your exquisite corpse is going to be a picture of fantastic animals, and the top part is going to be all the possible heads, draw a different head on each little page in the top part of the book. Then move down and draw

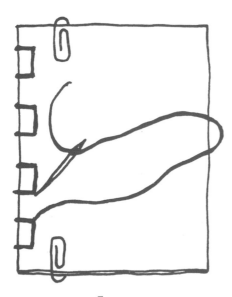

Figure 3

a different set of shoulders and front legs on each page of the second part, and so on. If your exquisite corpse is going to be a story, write a different setting on each page of the top part of your book, and so on. This is where your friends will come in handy! It's easier to think of this many ideas when you have more than one head to do the thinking!

13. When the exquisite corpse is finished, see how many combinations you can make. Fold the pages so that the top of page one is connected to the second part of page two and that page is connected to the tenth part of page three, and so on. Once your book is made, you and your friends will have lots of fun trying out all the different combinations!

Artists' Books

What kind of book can speed up time, leap off the page, turn itself inside out, hide a secret, unfold in 10 different ways, and flip in two directions at once? What kind of book can celebrate a thunderstorm, weep at the sorrow of a war torn country, make jokes and smooth away the stresses of modern life? An artist's book, that's what kind.

Some artists paint, while others photograph. Some artists sculpt in clay or in wood. Others draw with pen and ink. Book artists do all these things, but they do them in book form. Books let artists create not only spaces, shapes,

Gwen Diehn, page from *How to Fly in Dreams*, 1995.

and colors, but also time. Book artists make as many pictures as they need, then they arrange, fold, glue, or sew them so that the reader or viewer will see the pictures in a certain order and at a certain speed.

Book artist Susan Share makes hundreds of folds in some of her books so that when we watch her unfold them we see not only shapes and colors, but also waterfalls of graceful motion. The falling folds stir a light breeze and make a nice soft fluttering sound, too. Another artist, Keith Smith, creates books, such as *Book 91*, containing strings that cast shadows that play across the pages as they turn.

Some book artists use a flip book form to create quickly moving pictures. Ed Emberley is a writer and artist who has recently published a set of four flip books that show eight natural processes. When you flip through his books you can watch a butterfly emerge from a chrysalis, a hen lay an egg, and a tadpole develop into a frog.

Book artists use every material you can imagine to weave their magic spells in books. Here are a few examples: corn husks, transparent plastic sheets, wood, clay, copper foil, rope, all kinds of cloth, old books, grasses, bamboo, mirrors, and electric lights.

Many artists' books are one of a kind. Look for them where you find other art work in museums and galleries, or check the libraries of some large museums. Some artists' books have been printed and sold commercially. You can find these in museum shops and bookstores. There are artists' book centers in some cities, such as Pyramid Atlantic, located near Washington, D.C.; The Pacific Center for the Book Arts, in San Francisco; The Visual Studies Workshop, in Rochester, New York; and The Minnesota Center for the Book, in Minneapolis. These places show artists' books, and offer workshops in book arts. If you live near a book center, find out about taking a workshop. I am sure you would enjoy it!

Starburst

Do you have a collection of poems, jokes, stamps, pressed flowers, feathers, cartoons, or photographs? Here's a book that can hold your collection, and can give each flower or poem the chance to burst forth on center stage! This kind of book is called a lotus book, but it also looks like a starburst.

WHAT YOU NEED

- ✧ 6 to 10 sheets of white or colored copier paper, 8½ inches by 11 inches (22 by 28 cm)
- ✧ Scissors
- ✧ Glue stick
- ✧ 2 pieces of cardboard, each 4½ inches by 4½ inches (11 by 11 cm)
- ✧ 2 sheets of decorated cover paper, each 6 inches by 6 inches (15 by 15 cm)
- ✧ 1 piece of flat, thin ribbon, 2 feet (60 cm) long

WHAT YOU DO

1. Square each sheet of copier paper by folding it as shown in Figure 1. Cut off the leftover piece across the bottom of the triangle. Unfold the

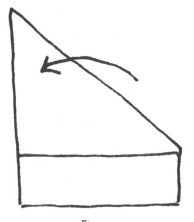

Figure 1

paper, and you should have a square with a crease going from one corner to the other.

2. Fold the paper square back along the crease, and press the fold with your finger to make it sharp.

3. Unfold the paper and fold it sharply in half from top to bottom. Press this crease. Keeping the paper folded, fold it in half the other way. Press the crease.

4. Unfold the paper. It should now have three creases. Fold it again along the diagonal (corner to corner) crease, but this time fold it the opposite way.

5. Open out the paper. You'll see four boxes made by the creases. Two of the boxes have diagonal creases and two don't. Pinch gently on the sides of the diagonal creases so that the two plain boxes fold up toward each other. See Figure 2.

6. Push the two diagonal folds toward the center and toward each other. You'll be able to flatten the two plain boxes over the creases. Repeat steps 2 through 6 for each sheet of copier paper.

7. To attach the pages to each other, place a folded piece of paper on the table in front of you in a diamond position. Keep the two folded edges to your left and the open, unfolded edges to your right.

8. Rub glue stick over the entire top sheet of the diamond. Place another diamond exactly on top of the first one, with the edges in the same position. Press down to glue the sheets together.

9. Repeat steps 7 and 8 until all the sheets are glued together.

10. Now you are ready to cover the two pieces of cardboard. Place one piece of cardboard in the center of a piece of decorated paper and draw its outline, then draw glue tabs. See Figure 3. Cut the cover paper along the outside of the tab lines.

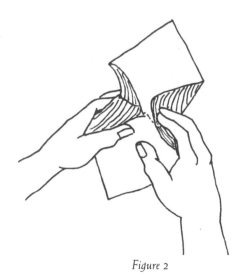

Figure 2

Figure 3

11. Put glue over the entire inside of the piece of cover paper. Carefully place the piece of cover cardboard inside its outline. Fold the glue tabs over and press down. Press down all over both sides of the cover so that the paper is glued flat with no bubbles. Repeat steps 10 and 11 for the other cover.

12. Place the two covers, right sides down, on a table with two of their corners ½ inch (1.5 cm) apart as shown in Figure 4. Rub a line of glue from corner to corner across the two covers. Place the ribbon across the glue line. Be sure to leave ½ inch (1.5 cm) between the two covers. See Figure 5.

13. Put glue all over the top sheet in the stack of glued pages and press it against the inside front cover. The ribbon will be sandwiched between the cover and the pages. Repeat this step with the back cover and pages.

14. When you open the book, the pages will burst open, giving you four places on each page for poems, jokes, drawings, pressed flowers, stamps, or whatever you have collected.

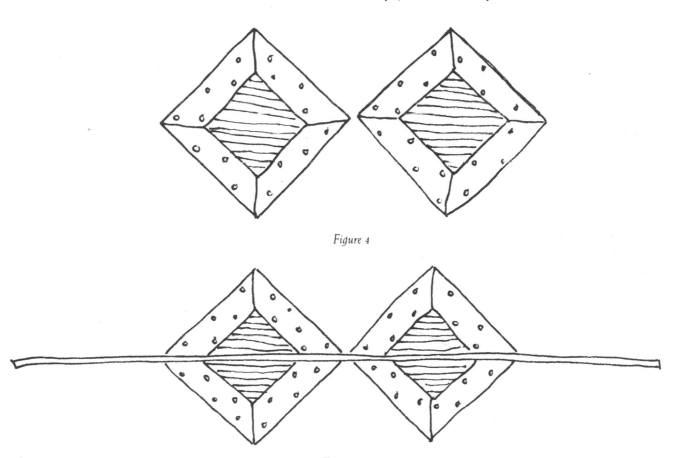

Figure 4

Figure 5

Acknowledgments

For help with this book I would like to thank, first of all, Deborah Morgenthal, my editor at Lark Books, who not only believed in the book from the very beginning, but cheered me on so unfailingly that she made writing and illustrating the book pure pleasure. Thanks also to Kathy Holmes, the art director who designed the book at Lark; she asked me for my ideas and then blended them gracefully with her own wonderful ones. I owe much gratitude to Elizabeth Earle and her students at The Learning Center in Black Mountain, North Carolina, and to Fran Loges and her students at Isaac Dickson School in Asheville, North Carolina, who field-tested projects, told me where the unclear instructions were, and gave me good advice for improving them. Many thanks also to my son Erik Diehn, who wrote text and illustrated a number of the model books and gave welcome moral support. And finally I thank Ruth C. Irwin, who kept me company while I worked on illustrations, and then contributed her own work in the calligraphy sample and illuminated letters.

Many, many thanks to the kids who helped us make and show off the projects:

Tashima Brown
Samuel Caldwell
Dana Detweiler
Katie Lynn Getchell
Parks and Grace Greene
Makai Laurin
Amanda McGrayne
Ashley Rhymer
Alice Royer
Lynnea Skiman
Cody Smith
Indy Smith
Adrian Tambor
Grace Welsh

Note: The *acknowledgments* section of a book is the place where you get to thank everybody who in any way helped you with the book, from your Aunt Mary, who gave you your first set of colored pencils, to your faithful cat Esmaralda, who slept on your desk the entire time you wrote the book. Not all books have an acknowledgments section, but you can choose to include one in any book that seems to have been helped along by other people.

Glossary

Accordion fold. A series of back and forth folds made in a long sheet of paper, like the bellows of an accordion.

Binding. The process used to hold pages within the covers of a book.

Codex. A book that is bound along one edge.

Coptic binding. Originally leather bindings made in Coptic monasteries in Egypt from as early as the fourth century A.D. This method of binding consists of sewing signatures to each other and to the cover boards with chain stitches. There is no spine board.

Endpapers. The pieces of paper that are glued to the insides of cover boards.

Foot. The outer bottom edge of a book.

Fore-edge. The outer edge of a book opposite the spine.

Glue binding. Holding the pages together within the cover boards with glue.

Gutter. In a pair of facing pages, the space where they are joined together.

Head. The top edge of the text block.

Pamphlet binding. A way of holding a single signature together within covers by sewing through three or sometimes five holes in the fold of the signature and cover.

Scoring. Making a crease in paper by pressing it so that the paper will fold more easily.

Signature. A group of pages that make up a section of a book.

Spine. A board that provides support for the back of the book.

Stab binding. A binding style in which front and back covers are attached to the text block by decorative stitching at the side.

Text block. The contents of the book, made up of all the signatures.

Index

Colophon

The text for this book was set in 12-point Weiss. Emil Weiss based his 1926 design for Weiss on Italian Renaissance typefaces. It is one of the earliest contemporary serif types, with vertical strokes that are wider on top than at the bottom. The project titles for this book were composed in 18-point Mylo Regular. Mylo Regular was created in 1996 by Eric Stevens. It is an original design created from analog sketches and then scanned and digitized in the computer. This book was created with Quark Express on a Power Macintosh computer.

The book was printed by Oceanic Graphic Printing Ltd. in Hong Kong on 115 gsm Japanese white A matt art paper (gsm=the number of grams in a square meter of paper). The text blocks were stitched together with colored thread. The spine of the book was covered in clear plastic so that the stitching would show.

A *colophon* is a statement at the end of a book that describes publication information, such as the typeface used, the kind of paper the book is printed on, the date the book was printed, the number of copies printed, who printed the book, what kind of binding was used, and so on. In artists' books the colophon often tells what fibers the paper was made of (if it was handmade paper), the reason the book was written, how the text was put into the book, how the illustrations were done, how many copies of the book were made, and which numbered copy this particular book is.

The first colophons appeared in hand-copied manuscript books as early as 827 AD. These early colophons described who copied the book, who illustrated or illuminated it, the title of the book, and the date and place of its copying. Sometimes these early colophons included a blessing for the client who commissioned the book. After the invention of the printing press, colophons told the date of the printing and the typeface used, as well as how and by whom the type was set and the book was printed.